blue
rider
press

ALWAYS PACK A PARTY DRESS

Also by Amanda Brooks

I Love Your Style

ALWAYS PACK
A PARTY DRESS

AND

OTHER LESSONS LEARNED FROM A (HALF) LIFE IN FASHION

AMANDA BROOKS

BLUE RIDER PRESS

AN IMPRINT OF PENGUIN RANDOM HOUSE
NEW YORK

blue
rider
press

An imprint of Penguin Random House LLC
375 Hudson Street
New York, New York 10014

Library of Congress Cataloging-in-Publication Data

Brooks, Amanda.
Always pack a party dress : and other lessons learned from a (half) life in fashion / Amanda Brooks.
p.   cm.
ISBN 978-0-399-17083-6
1. Brooks, Amanda. 2. Brooks, Amanda—Philosophy. 3. Women fashion designers—United States—
Biography. 4. Fashion designers—United States—Biography. 5. Fashion design—New York (State)—
New York. 6. Conduct of life. I. Title.
TT505.B77A3   2015   014049923
746.9' 2092—dc23
[B]

Printed in the United States of America
1   3   5   7   9   10   8   6   4   2

Book design by Richard Pandiscio, William Loccisano / Pandiscio Co.

*Penguin is committed to publishing works of quality and integrity.
In that spirit, we are proud to offer this book to our readers;
however, the story, the experiences, and the words
are the author's alone.*

*To Coco—
for all the adventures,
fashion and otherwise,
that lie ahead of you.*

*To Zach—
for always knowing
exactly what to say.*

*To Christopher—
for so faithfully standing
next to me.*

CONTENTS

ALWAYS PACK
A PARTY DRESS

INTRODUCTION

SITTING HERE at the kitchen table in our farmhouse, dressed in jodhpurs and muddy boots, just in from a morning ride, I am trying to remind myself how and why I decided to write this book. It's been three years since I took a break from my twenty-year career in fashion to spend a yearlong creative sabbatical at my husband's family farm in the English countryside. Yes, we're still here. And while I have many ideas about what my professional future might hold, many of which include fashion, it's hard to imagine making anywhere else my home.

But back to where this book began. The very first idea came to me as do many of my ideas: at the end of a long walk. It was early 2010, and I was in Manhattan, walking from my Lower East Side apartment to pick up my kids from school in Greenwich Village. I was reflecting on the positive feedback I had received after writing on my blog about cutting off all my hair at age twenty-two. The anecdote included typical coming-of-age optimism, a large dose of humility, some fabulous fashion-world people, my parents, and some pretty heavy questioning of who I was and why people liked me.

Opposite: In the kitchen of our home on Fairgreen Farm, shortly after the move. I'm wearing an Isabel Marant jumpsuit and Céline espadrilles.

I liked writing the story and the similar ones that followed. I liked putting a human face on the glamour and exclusivity of the fashion world. I liked writing in order to revisit the moments, the people, the experiences that had shaped me throughout my time in the fashion industry. I liked recognizing that in many ways, the fashion world has escorted me from an intern in my teenage years, to accessories designer as a young adult, to creative director as I became a wife, to fashion director as I discovered my role as a mother, and eventually to who I am today.

At the time, these thoughts weren't a book. They were a direction for my blog, which fell to the side pretty soon after, when I accepted a job as Barneys' fashion director and agreed to set aside my personal work and social media pursuits. But as my time in that role came to an end, I started thinking about writing a follow-up book to *I Love Your Style* and wondered what that might be. When I first wrote that book, it had felt like the first in a series—*I Love Your* [Kids', Wedding, Home, Men's] *Style* could easily follow. But now that the idea of collaging well-researched photos from every decade has been adapted by Pinterest and Tumblr, I realized the intrigue of that format, for me at least, had come and gone. Friends in the publishing industry agreed, and there I was, left to start from scratch.

A couple of months before I left Barneys, I revisited the idea of writing down these stories about coming of age in the fashion industry. It was important to me that I had something to work on next. I couldn't wait to get back to writing. As damn hard as it is at times, I thrive on the singular creative perspective, the flexible hours, and the processing of ideas, thoughts, and emotions that writing provides. So I called a friend who was an editor at a publishing house I admired and ran some ideas by her. None of them particularly resonated with her. As I was listening to her feedback, I remembered the personal fashion stories I had so enjoyed writing for my blog, and suggested that perhaps they could be compiled into a book. Without hesitation, she told me this was my next project.

18

It wouldn't be until nine months later that I sat down to start writing. After moving my family across the Atlantic, settling the kids into our home and a new school, and setting up life (Wi-Fi!) on a remote farm, I couldn't have felt further from fashion. My days were spent taking photographs, doing the school run, cooking family meals, riding horses, making jam, and updating what had been our summer house for year-round living. I was in full decompression-from-New-York mode and was giving myself permission to follow my bliss. It was hard to want to think about fashion and all that I had purposely taken a break from, and I started to doubt my new book idea, which had once seemed so promising. But there is something exhilarating and empowering about going in the direction of my fear, in the direction of the thing that seems hard, and so I slowly began to write more about my experience in fashion. It was over the winter, as the stories continued and evolved, that I began to realize how important and integral this reflection on my time in the industry was to seeing clearly and understanding how I had gone—for the time being—from an NYC girl devoted to her career to a stay-at-home mom on a farm in the middle of nowhere. It has shown me how everything I have done so far in my life has led to new challenges, to deep happiness, to the chance to take everything I have learned and accomplished and apply that to whatever it is I decide to do next.

In order for me to write anything, whether it be an article or a blog post or a book, I have to be able to picture who I am talking to and understand why I am telling them this story. Although the process of writing, especially in the case of this book, is always beneficial to me in some way, it is not written for me, at least not me in the present tense. So who is this book for? I think of my little sister Phoebe, who recently graduated from college with a degree in integrative media. She spent her last unemployed summer waitressing while sending her résumé to anyone who was hiring in a creative field even remotely related to her interests and wondering what her future might hold. She had so many questions: "Do I have to decide right now what I want to do for my career?

Opposite: My office is in an old garden shed, so the wood burner is key to making it cozy. I bought the leopard stool at a local antiques shop for $150.

21

Or will my fate be decided by the job I happen to get?" "Do I even want to get a real job? Or can I go freelance right away?" I am proud to say that as I was writing this book, she got hired as a graphic designer with a high-profile New York marketing, advertising, and trend-forecasting firm. It's right on target with her talent and her education. Hopefully she will like it, but it's entirely possible that the company will be too big or too corporate for her taste, despite the comfy paycheck. She may decide she wants to become a film animator or work at a magazine in eighteen months' time. But the only way she will know is by trying something and seeing if she likes it. If she doesn't, she can cross that off the list and try something else. It seems simple, but I've seen countless people—myself included—become paralyzed by the notion that they should know exactly what and who they want to be right out of college. Although this book is about my experience in the fashion industry, I hope it will transcend fashion and also be inspiring to any young man or woman, like Phoebe, who is launching into their career and wondering how to get from A to B, how to figure out what they want to be "when they grow up," how to cope with more success than they imagined or more disappointment than they think they can handle.

I also think about the young girls I met in the Beverly Hills office of William Morris Endeavor, an L.A.–based talent agency, when I worked as the company's fashion director. Those girls were so in awe of fashion, so enamored of it. But at the same time, they were intimidated by—or, more likely, scared as hell of—the prospect of even approaching it. I didn't see these girls as being much different than I was at their age; if anything they were more sophisticated in their early twenties than I had been. But fashion was this ultraexclusive, behind-the-velvet-rope world to them.

My former research intern Chelsea Fairless, who now edits VFILES.

And so I hope this book will make fashion seem a little more forgiving and user-friendly to young women and men who want to take part in it, now or in the future. You might think to yourself, "Oh, but not every girl gets to meet Diane von Furstenberg at age eighteen and have her as a mentor." And you would be right—not every girl does. But anyone who is talented and works hard and makes their way in the fashion industry has a story about someone like DVF who is a hero to them, and takes an interest in them, and guides them along.

My former assistant Laura Stoloff, who is the senior market editor at WSJ Magazine.

Chelsea and Laura, twentysomethings who worked for me throughout the different phases in my career, also came to mind while I was writing this book. Both girls were new to New York City when they started with me, and I watched them each reconcile who they were and where they had come from with where they wanted to go and who they wanted to be. They each had different personalities with different goals, but they were both trying to make their way toward having a career in fashion. The story of how Chelsea came to work for me is impressive. I was looking for an intern to help me with photo research for *I Love Your Style*, so I placed an ad on the Parsons The New School for Design website. A nice girl named Megan sent me a good résumé, and I met her and thought she would do the job well. But the day before I planned to hire her, I got a letter and résumé from a girl called Chelsea Fairless. Good name, right? Something about her note made me want to meet her. She told me she had read, cover to cover, every single issue of *Vogue* since she was twelve years old. So she came over that evening to chat. She had *so much* desire and enthusiasm to work for me. The first thing

she said to me was that she knew every picture of me that had ever been published in a magazine or a newspaper. At this point I was torn between thinking she was a creepy stalker or a thoroughly devoted fan of fashion. But she impressed me with her in-depth and historical knowledge of both fashion and photography—after all, I was looking for a researcher—and so I decided to give her a go. I'd like to think Chelsea learned a lot from working for me, but in truth, it's possible that I learned more from her. She is now senior editor at VFILES, a hip, downtown fashion media company where she is thriving.

From Laura, I learned how much people have the capacity to grow and learn and blossom. While I was impressed during my interview with Laura, once I hired her, she was so nervous she could barely answer the phone! I started to have doubts. She was so nice and smart and stylish, and her résumé was so perfectly suited to the job I had offered her, but my expectations were high. As much as I liked her personally, the first year was a little bumpy, especially because I switched jobs in the middle of it. But eventually, with hard work and dedication on her part, and patience and guidance on mine, Laura hit her stride. And then some. She became a cracking good assistant to me and contributed creatively to many of my most ambitious projects following both my own career goals and those as a consultant to other companies. When I eventually landed at Barneys, I fought tooth and nail to bring Laura with me, and she eventually became the assistant fashion director there. She is now the senior market editor at *WSJ Magazine*, and I am so proud of her.

So what could I share with all these girls and young women in my thoughts? What could I impart to the twentysomething version of myself still lurking somewhere inside of me? And what could I write down now that might be relevant to my daughter in not so many years? I certainly don't want to give anyone advice. This book is not a career guide or any kind of comprehensive memoir. It's just my experience. These stories are the memorable moments, the straight lines and the crossroads of setting goals and sometimes

meeting them and sometimes moving away from them. They're the lessons *I* learned and how I learned them. I don't pretend to have had any kind of wisdom when making many of the big decisions in this book, but when I look back now over my first twenty years in fashion, I feel that it all kind of worked out pretty well in the end.

And how can I reflect on my life so far in fashion without sharing the most important sartorial lessons I have learned? How I figured out that I usually look best when I do my own hair and makeup? How I packed for three weeks of nonstop fashion shows? How I learned to mix multiple denim pieces in one look? And how much fun I've had exploring fashion and coming up with all kinds of new looks—some of which hit the bull's-eye, others of which were complete belly flops? As a general rule, I tend to share how I figured things out and let you do the same for yourself. I'm not so into strict fashion rules—who am I to tell you what works for you? But I do love to share my inspiration, and in this book, as in *I Love Your Style* and on my blog, there is plenty of it, including the people, the places, and the designers who have most inspired me.

Alongside the fashion lessons learned, there is the evolution of my own personal style. All of you who read *I Love Your Style* know that I have never felt shame in being a chameleon when it comes to defining myself and my style through clothes. Throughout my life, I have tried out nearly every major and minor trend you can think of. I've been decorative, I've been minimal, I've worn wide flares and skinny jeans, I've had my hair cut from a one-inch, Jean Seberg style to all the way down my back and every length in between. I gained a lot of wisdom from all those phases, but as I entered my forties, and as my life in England had encouraged me to focus and simplify my style, I was left with one question: Which one of those girls is me? I don't know if I ever would have found that answer living in New York City. There is too much inspiration, too much to try on, too many people other than myself to please in order to answer that question honestly and succinctly. However, it took no time to answer that question as soon as I moved to the farm.

Packing for life in England was an exercise in discipline and

restraint, but it wasn't as challenging as you might think. There were some pretty simple parameters. I have one small closet and a wardrobe that has six small drawers and some limited additional hanging space. I expanded my storage capacity a bit by buying storage boxes for under the bed and to store in the barn (for out-of-season clothes). But still, I had reduced twenty years of manic clothes-collecting to three suitcases when I boarded the plane to move here. I took all the things I knew I'd wear on a daily basis— T-shirts, men's tailored buttondowns, cozy sweaters, jeans and cor- duroys, boots. And then I added some fashion favorites I couldn't resist—my Alaïa skirts, a Chanel motorcycle jacket, all my classic sportswear from Céline, my feminine bohemian pieces from Isabel Marant. I knew I wouldn't need to dress up that often here, but when I did, I would want to look my best, so I packed three killer evening looks, including a black-and-white beaded chiffon dress by Proenza Schouler, two pairs of Manolo Blahnik BB pumps (black and brown suede), my woven satin Bottega Veneta clutch, a vintage Oscar de la Renta evening jacket, and a Phillip Lim em- broidered cape. As soon as I unpacked, I had a new and clearly defined image of myself through my clothes. I am mostly classic, in a pared-down, almost minimalist way, with a touch of romantic bohemianism and a dash of high fashion. There is also a certain sense of preppiness in my plaid flannel shirts, my ivory fisherman's sweater, and my fleece Patagonia jacket. These pieces aren't influ- enced by a fashion trend, but by my childhood in Palm Beach and Westchester. This return to my roots brings a great feeling of true self to my style. I feel at home in these clothes. This whole picture of the more clearly defined "me" makes sense of all the years of experimentation through trial and error, and also gives me greater self-confidence in where I've come from, the journey I have taken to get here, and the result: where I am today.

And finally, please don't feel that you should read this book in chronological order from front to back all in one sitting. When I read books of stories like these, I like to read just one chapter in the bath each night and spend the following day reflecting on it.

Opposite, clockwise from top left: My very useful Céline three-pocket purse bought at the outlet store. My Céline trench that I live in, also found at the outlet. My favorite bag, a Proenza Schouler PS1. Snakeskin Céline sandals; the heel is just the right height.

Or maybe you just want to pick it up from time to time to look at the pictures, and choose a random chapter that resonates with you at that moment. My hope is that you'll like a photo or relate to a story or feel encouraged to try something new in your career or your style, or possibly even take a moment to consider your future. It's not as scary as it sounds. I promise.

Opposite, clockwise from top left: My Rag & Bone military jacket. My favorite summer dress from J.Crew. This Céline blazer reminds me of how my mom dressed in the early eighties. A Thakoon dress that always stays in the front of my closet.

IS THERE ANY better compliment than a friend saying, "That is so *you*!" It's the double whammy of a feel-good sartorial pat on the back—not only is it implying that your friend knows you well enough to know what *you* is, but it also suggests that you, in fact, know yourself well enough to project what *you* is.

But how do we get to know who that *you* is? Besides the everyday trial and error we face as we buy clothes, wear them, show them to our friends, see what our husbands think, and find out if we'll ever wear them again, and if so how often, there is also the mandatory task of exposing ourselves to and reacting to inspiration.

Inspiration has always been my number one means of fashion evolution and self-knowledge, even though it's always changing. When I was in my early twenties with my weekends still to myself, I spent hours putting together scrapbooks filled with magazine tear sheets of women, clothes, homes, places, art, photographs, and anything else that grabbed my attention and made me want to fold the page down. I also included personal photographs, cool ticket stubs, beautifully designed party invitations, letters in elegant handwriting, and so on. At the time, I did this exercise for the fun of it, but now I can look back at that time and see, visually, who *I* was then.

These days, in order to see who I am now, I always keep a "scrapboard" in my office. It's a living, breathing thing that changes all the time—one picture comes down, another tear sheet goes up. As I am writing this, it is plastered with S/S '13 Céline ads; printed Instagram photos of my kids; my place card from a lunch at Diane von Furstenberg's house, hand-drawn by DVF herself; a postcard of my favorite John Currin painting; a vintage picture of an anonymous, eccentrically dressed woman; an invitation to the tenth anniversary celebration of Daylesford, our local farm shop in England; some tear-outs from an old Isabel Marant catalogue; and a wristband from a New Year's Coldplay/Jay Z concert. My board is filled with all my favorite visual reminders, and sometimes when I am stuck creatively, I look to it to borrow an idea or two from the people, places, and things that inspire me most. It reminds me of where I came from, who I am, and who I want to be.

Opposite: The inspiration wall in my office, which changes almost weekly.

EMBRACE YOUR HISTORY

I SPENT MOST of my twenties trying to subvert the fact that I was a WASP. I bought so many ugly things—futuristic green suede Prada Sport sneakers, iridescent purple lipstick from Chanel, and a bolero jacket from a thrift store that looked like it had turquoise grass growing on it—in an effort to make myself look less preppy. I remember when Jimmy Paul was doing my hair for my wedding. I chose him because he was a friend but also because he was "editorial," meaning he had created many of the high-fashion hairstyles for *Vogue* and for the models on the runways of the best designer shows. But ironically, all Jimmy wanted to do was make me look like Grace Kelly on my wedding day. "Not toooooo tasteful," I repeated over and over again, when he wanted to coif my hair into a perfect side-parted chignon. He knew me well enough to push me (even though it was my wedding day), and we went back and forth until we agreed on a Spanish-inspired center part and braided bun. Perfect. Still classic, but with a little bit of the exotic thrown in.

I also remember going to my parents' club for Saturday night dinner during those years. This was WASP central, with men in printed pants and ladies in colorful cardigans. I would do anything not to fit in—I'd wear ridiculously high platform shoes, oversize chandelier ear-rings, or a sundress with Chanel logos printed all over it (logos are a country club no-no). What a show-off I was! Anyway, after I got married and had kids in my late twenties, I settled myself down a bit and started to think about clothes differently. It was too exhausting to try so hard to reinvent my look all the time. I also started to feel like when I dressed in clothes that were familiar to my life and my history, I felt more comfortable, more like myself. It's exhausting to try to be someone other than who you are. Not to say that in order to be yourself you have to dress a certain way. But for me, to embrace who I am and where I came from and to combine that with all that I had learned in my years of intense fashion experimentation gave me the sense of wholeness that I craved and hadn't felt in a long time.

Opposite: Heading to an Erdem show in London wearing a Céline outfit (+ J.Crew jeans) that embraces my classic roots.

WHERE I'M
COMING FROM

1974—Born in Palm Beach, Florida, second of two girls. Lived in a relatively modest house right on the beach that my grandfather, an architect, built for my parents as a wedding present. Mom and Dad had matching Belgian Shoes loafers and gold St. Christopher's medallions.

1977—Parents split up. My mom, my sister Kim, and I moved to a condo in West Palm, right across from a Puerto Rican bakery that had the best flan. Walked in my first fashion show for Lilly Pulitzer.

1979—Mom got remarried and we moved to Bronxville, New York, a conservative, *Stepford Wives* suburb of New York City. Walked to the local public school every morning with my new BFF, Alexandra. Entered the era of eighties preppy sportswear.

1980—Joined the local gymnastics team and wanted to look like all the Yonkers girls with feathered hair and blue eyeliner. What I most envied, though, was that they were allowed to chew gum. Continued to spend summers and holidays with my dad in Palm

Opposite: My childhood friend Alexandra Kerr and me playing dress-up in our rented summer house in Quogue, 1979. I'd be perfectly happy to dress like that now.

35

Beach. An opera singer friend of his bought me red Ray-Bans for my birthday and I didn't take them off for months.

1983—Discovered Esprit and Merona at my local Gimbels department store. Loved the preppy stripes and colors mixed with more fashion-relevant shapes.

1984—Got braces and my first pair of Guess jeans—blue denim with purple pinstripes and ankle zips. Spent the first of many Saturdays dressed up like Madonna.

1985—For middle school graduation, Mom and I designed a dress together, bought fabric at Laura Ashley, and had the dress made by a local seamstress. I wanted it to be strapless, but Mom insisted on spaghetti straps. She was right.

1986—Went to summer camp in Maine. Caught in the middle of a changing sense of identity, I couldn't find a group of girls to fit in with. The cool, preppy girls wore Bermuda shorts and polo shirts, and I got teased for my fold-and-roll jeans and my Michael Jackson sweatshirt.

1987—Mom's fortieth birthday. She wore Vicky Tiel couture. I wore Laura Ashley. Again. Transferred to Horace Mann, a private high school in Riverdale filled with New York City kids of a whole other breed than I was used to. Showed up on my first day, dressed by my older sister Kim, in head-to-toe Benetton and white leather Keds. Fit right in.

1989—Had the summer of my life in Palm Beach. Waterskiing camp during the day, Bartles & Jaymes wine coolers on the beach at night. Discovered thrift shopping and got a whole new wardrobe at the Animal Rescue League charity shop—beaded cashmere cardigans, ripped 501s, leopard shoes. Went to Deerfield Academy, a WASPy New England boarding school in the fall.

From top: Mom and Dad in Palm Beach, 1972; my mom still has that ostrich Gucci bag. Hanging with pals in Florida, 1970s. Alexandra and me in Bronxville, 1979. With my "Brownies" friends, 1982. Ice skating with Alexandra, 1983; it was all about the pom-poms. Learning to dive in my Florence Eisman swimsuit, Gulf Stream, Florida, 1984.

1990—First Grateful Dead concert. Long, floral Putumayo skirts replaced the Laura Ashley ones. That summer Dad made me shine and polish my perfectly worn L.L. Bean camp mocs to go to the Palm Beach Bath and Tennis Club for lunch. Trauma.

1991—New boyfriend from NYC. Tried to make my look more sophisticated. Bought Joan & David loafers and Ann Taylor jackets. Discovered the high-end outlet mall in Paramus, New Jersey. Made my "society debut" at the Westchester Cotillion in a dress designed by my mom.

1992—Graduated from Deerfield in a Ralph Lauren dress I bought on final sale from Lord & Taylor. Arrived at Brown. Overwhelmed by girls dressed in Chanel and Marc Jacobs. Found solace at Contempo Casuals. Met Diane von Furstenberg while briefly dating her son, Alex.

1993—Dated preppy/hippie childhood friend Andrew, who went to UVM. Went to more Phish concerts than I would have cared to and rediscovered my bohemian side.

1994—My attention came back to fashion. Started working as a studio assistant at Patrick Demarchelier. Discovered Zara.

1996—Graduated from college. Cut off all of my hair. Got hired at Gagosian. Embraced the nineties "gallerina" uniform of all-black fitted sportswear and bootcut trousers.

1997—Met Christopher. Went to Paris with him, where I attended my first (and only) Chanel couture show where I actually had a seat. Got photographed by *Vogue* for the first time. Spent all my disposable income at Ghost, Calypso, and Zara.

1998—Moved into my first solo NYC apartment on Jones Street. Obsessively visited the flea market on weekends with my neighbor Plum Sykes. Started collecting vintage handbags.

From top: Wearing Esprit at my roller skating / Cabbage Patch Kid birthday party, 1985. Sporting my new Merona look in Palm Beach, 1985. Feeling cool in Benetton and Ray Bans, 1986. Channeling Madonna with Danielle, 1988.

1999—Left Gagosian. Accepted a job at Fekkai. Traveled to Paris—a lot. Lived in a pair of Stephane Kélian hunter green suede stiletto boots that were a gift from Christopher.

2000—Got lured away from Fekkai to Hogan. Spent the millennium New Year camping on a plain in Kenya with Christopher and friends from Nairobi. Fell in love with the bohemian romance of English expats living in Africa.

2001—Got pregnant and married, in that order. Dismissed idea of a formal engagement ring in favor of a Chanel celestial double-star ring. Shifted work to a freelance basis and included Tuleh in my daily schedule. Gave birth to Coco. Moved to big, raw loft on Chrystie Street. Overwhelmed by the task of decorating, we lived out of boxes for nearly a year.

2003—Gave birth to son, Zach. As a baby present, Tuleh designer Bryan Bradley gave me a red leather Chloé bag with heavy metal chain straps intended to function as a diaper bag.

2004—Moved on from Tuleh. Set up an office across the hall from our apartment on Chrystie Street. Spent most days in "cozy clothes," only changing into a real outfit for out-of-office meetings.

2005-2007—Set about writing *I Love Your Style* and pretended I was a full-time writer, even though I could manage to write for only three hours a day. Freed from being attached to any one brand, borrowed clothes from every designer imaginable and experimented with different fashion styles.

2007—Founded Amanda Brooks Inc. Began to feel less interested in trends and more concerned with making wise, timeless investments in clothes.

From top: Alexandra and I both wearing Laura Ashley at our lower school graduation, 1986. Playing dress-up with Elyse and Danielle at a bar mitzvah, 1987. Celerie and I still into Laura Ashley, 1988. Kimberly, Nicole, and me in our new wicker hats, Palm Beach, 1989.

2009—Earned enough money to buy designer clothes for the first time. Began to grow restless raising two kids in NYC.

2010—Became fashion director of William Morris Endeavor. Spent a lot of time in Los Angeles. Had fantasies about the laid-back, bohemian/suburban lifestyle. Made Christopher fly out to look at houses with me.

2011—Let go of L.A. dreams when I got hired at Barneys. Made a deal with myself that if I could last five years at Barneys, I would give myself a year off living on our farm in England as a reward.

2012—Personal and professional worlds came to a head. Overwhelmed by realization that now was the right time for me (and my family) to leave New York, decided to move to England ahead of schedule. Winnowed the contents of two walk-in closets and ten storage trunks down to three suitcases. Lost ten pounds and broke out in shingles when leaving my job and moving my family across the Atlantic coincided.

2013—Felt an overwhelming sense of balance and peace as life was scaled way back and I focused on the things I cared about most. Learned to make jam. Started quest for the perfect Wellington boot and vintage tweed riding jacket.

2014—Decide to stay in England for the time being. Visit New York often and realize it's always there when I need it to be.

From top: In my custom-made Cotillion dress with my escort, Jeff McDowell, 1992. Headed to Wimbledon, 1999. Celebrating the millenium in Tracy Feith tie-dye, 2000. With my girlfriends at my first Vogue *party, 2000. In Chanel at Coco's christening, England, 2001.*

MY MOTHER

I HAVE ALWAYS chosen different style icons for different times or aspects of my life—high-fashion ones, casual ones, tomboy ones, uber feminine ones, glamorous ones, subtle ones—but the one style icon who seems to serve me most consistently and most comprehensively is my mother. I've spoken a lot in the past about my love of the iconic American sportswear—the shift dress, the Bill Blass suit, the perfectly pressed shorts, the striped shirts—my mom wore in Palm Beach in the sixties and the high fashions like Alaïa, Carolyne Roehm, and Vicky Tiel she wore in the eighties. But at this point in my life I am most intrigued by what my mom wears now in her sixties. First of all, I look a lot like my mom—both in silhouette and in facial features—so her path from her early forties to where she is now is informative and gives me an idea of where I am headed. But beyond that, I can relate to how she evolved toward a place where she spends less time and money on her clothes, and I look at her and aspire to be half as chic as she is even though her life is so much more dynamic than thinking about what to wear all the time. When we are in the Adirondacks every August, the vast majority of what my mom wears has been hanging in her closet for twenty years. There are the basics—the flannel plaid shirts, the hiking boots, the waterproof Tevas (which have finally come back into fashion!), the skinny corduroys, the cardigans, the rain jackets, and her signature "crusher" fishing hat adorned with fishing license pins. Then there are the fashion pieces—a red suede fringed jacket, a red lizard western belt from Billy Martin's (remember that store on Madison Ave?), and a dramatic vintage red paisley shawl. Yes, she loves red. And then each summer she'll add a half dozen new pieces—a J.Crew embroidered tunic, a new pair of jeans, striped loafer-shaped espadrilles among them that all work seamlessly with what she already has. Although my mom's look is the culmination of decades of trial and error, of collecting clothes, of evolving her lifestyle and adapting her style to suit her age, the effect appears confident, graceful, and effortless. What more could I want for myself?

Opposite: My mom, Liz Stewart, wearing Jax (the chic sportswear brand of the day) in Palm Beach, early 1960s.

MY TEENAGE YEARS: BOARDING SCHOOL, THE ADIRONDACKS, THE GRATEFUL DEAD, AND J.CREW

PATAGONIA jackets, long floral skirts, tweed jackets, Adidas Stan Smith sneakers, batik-print cotton shirts, blue blazers, Mexican hippie bracelets, fisherman's sweaters—these are all the things I thought I'd leave far behind once I left boarding school. When I was at Deerfield, my style was influenced by my preppy friends, my obsession with J.Crew, my love of the Grateful Dead, and the sporty outdoors hiking look I wore during my summers in the Adirondacks. Towards the end of college, I swore off the boho preppy look for good. But over the years, fashion has led me back to those days. Proenza Schouler made chunky-knit sweaters and quilted jackets cool again, Isabel Marant reintroduced the Indian-inspired romantic cotton florals, Phoebe Philo and Marc Jacobs resurrected Stan Smiths, Tory Burch revived the Mexican beach hippie look, and J.Crew gave prep school chic a much-needed boost. This new influx of enthusiasm for a look I know all too well has inspired me to embrace my own history and wear those things again with renewed enthusiasm.

Opposite: Wearing my favorite batik shirt and JanSport backpack, and carrying my Ray-Ban aviators at age fifteen in the Adirondacks.

*Clockwise from top left: At Deerfield Academy, 1989. Wearing Patagonias in the Adirondacks, 1995.
My mom's best friend, Mimi, in the Adirondacks, 1980. Mom's Teva's become relevant again, 2014.
My stepdad, Will, at Pomfret, 1954. Mom's preppy accessories, 2012.*

Clockwise from top left: My adult Adirondack style, 2010, photographed by Claibourne Swanson Frank. Jenna Lyons and her brother Ben in classic tomboy tailoring. My sister Kimberly and me at Deerfield, 1999. In the Adirondacks in a Proenza Schouler T-shirt, 2012. My stepdad, Will, with his cousins in the Adirondacks, 1940s. A 1990s J.Crew catalogue.

ALWAYS PACK
A PARTY DRESS

WHEN I WAS TWENTY years old, I dreamed of being a waitress in Burlington, Vermont, for the summer. My then boyfriend, Andrew, who went to UVM, was planning to spend the summer there, and I felt I was old enough to live with him and have a "normal" job. During the previous two summers, I'd done what my parents had encouraged me to do and what most kids in my circle had done: worked an internship in New York City. It was common wisdom that the most likely way to land a plum job after college was to have one or two career-relevant "work experiences" under your belt by the time you graduated.

In this regard, I was already ahead of the game. At age eighteen, I'd landed a job working for Laurie Jones, then the managing editor of *New York* magazine. I did some administrative work and gained an understanding of how a magazine was run, but essentially I spent much of my time writing up my personal views on New England boarding schools for Ms. Jones, whose sons were about to embark on the secondary school admissions process. I also had my first-ever sighting of a fashion editor. Her name was Martha Baker and she was the fashion director of the magazine.

Opposite: A portrait of me by Oberto Gili for Town & Country, *1996.*

47

She was blond and thin and beautiful and at least six feet tall. She would walk purposefully through the office in, say, a fitted white sheath dress that accentuated her perfect tan. She was impossibly glamorous and intimidating. I never once had the chance to speak to her, but I was in awe of her. (I should mention that more than a decade later, I would actually meet Martha on Shelter Island and am proud to now call her my friend. She is every bit as fabulous as she always was but is much less intimidating than my first impression led me to believe.)

I spent the following summer at Fine Line Features, the indie department of New Line Cinema. The highlight of my internship was working on post-production and promotional materials for Robert Altman's *Short Cuts* and Gus Van Sant's *Even Cowgirls Get the Blues*. My boss thought I looked enough like Uma Thurman to show up at a film screening wearing Uma's cowgirl costume to promote the film. Even just impersonating an actress gave me a thrill.

It was Presidents' Day weekend of 1994 when I drove to New York from Brown in my hand-me-down 1984 Ford Country Squire station wagon (complete with wood siding that had begun to peel) to have dinner with my parents and discuss summer plans. I wasn't sure how they'd react to my waitressing ambitions—I thought at best the chances were fifty-fifty that they'd be behind it. As I already had two unpaid internships under my belt, I thought they might be cool with the prospect of my actually earning some money. Generally speaking, I was an ambitious, even precocious teen, but there was a part of me that was just a suburban girl-next-door who wanted to do what most kids my age were doing.

That Friday night, we went to dinner at my parents' local hangout, a French bistro called Demarchelier on Eighty-Sixth Street and Madison. We knew the maître d', Michael, well, and he was used to me pestering him about how often the owner's brother, famed fashion photographer Patrick Demarchelier, ate there. At the time, I was finishing my sophomore year as a double major in art history and visual arts. I had wanted to major in visual arts with a focus on photography, but my mom felt strongly that my

time at an Ivy League school wouldn't be best spent making art full-time. So we compromised by agreeing that I could major in art as long as I double-majored in something more academic (I chose art history).

My interest in photography came from my stepfather, William. It was his weekend hobby, and he gave me my first camera—a Pentax K1000—and taught me how to develop and print photos in the darkroom he'd built in our basement. I would spend hours in there as a kid, developing negatives, mixing chemicals, and making prints. In high school, my love of photography was more art-based and academic—landscapes, portraits, etc. But by the time I was a sophomore, surrounded by fashion-obsessed friends and their subscriptions to *Vogue* and *Harper's Bazaar*, my interest in photography leaned toward fashion, and Patrick Demarchelier was one of my idols. He had photographed most of *Vogue*'s covers in the eighties and then most of *Bazaar*'s in the early nineties.

As we were seated at my parents' favorite round corner table at Demarchelier that February, Michael came over to tell me that Patrick and his family were seated at a nearby table, and that he'd be happy to walk me over and introduce me. My face flushed even thinking about it, and I nervously turned him down. I knew I had to go speak to Patrick, and that I would, in my own way and in my own time, but I needed a few minutes to get my courage up. I remember what I was wearing—black flared pants and a white ruffled blouse from Contempo Casuals. Fashion was having a hippie moment, and to keep up with my more glamorous, affluent college friends, I bought fashion knockoffs at the mall.

With growing pressure from my parents to seize the moment and introduce myself, I stood up from my chair and walked right past Patrick's table and straight into the ladies' room. My face was even more flushed—a mixture of nerves, embarrassment, and a few sips of my mom's red wine—and to make it worse, I was growing out my home-cut bangs. I have never been a girl to pass up an opportunity, but I really did feel inhibited. For what was probably five minutes but felt like thirty, I just couldn't pick myself up and

get going. With the thought that he might leave before I got the chance to say hello as motivation, I felt my body moving toward the bathroom door before my mind had the chance to catch up.

I made a beeline for the table. "Hi, my name is Amanda, and I'm a photography major in college. I'm a big fan of your work."

Patrick thanked me in a heavy French accent, and when he continued to speak, I had trouble understanding his rapid-fire, broken English. He tried again. Still nothing. I nodded politely, trying to look like I knew what he was saying. Finally, his wife, Mia, leaned toward me and said, "Patrick is inviting you to visit his studio tomorrow to watch a photo shoot."

"Oh, yes, that would be great. I would love to. Thank you," I said in a high-pitched, nervous tone that made me sound five years younger. Again, Mia translated the arrangements and wrote down the studio address on a piece of paper.

The next morning I awoke to a foot of fresh snow on the ground and more on the way. I left the house with plenty of time to make it from the Upper East Side down to Patrick's Chelsea studio on the 6 train, but as I walked out the door, my mom came running down the hall to warn me that the subways had just been shut down for the day. I don't even remember now how I ended up getting to Patrick's studio, but I do remember that I was a half hour late. I was mortified.

As I stepped onto the freight elevator, the super told me Patrick's studio was actually closed because of the blizzard but that Patrick was in his office on the floor below. I walked into the cavernous, white, loft-like space to find Patrick sitting alone at his desk. The wall behind him was covered floor to ceiling with his most iconic photos, all immaculately framed. And there was no translator.

Oh, no.

I sat down nervously and looked around at the photos mounted gallery-like on the wall—Stephanie Seymour hanging from a tree in St. Barts, a personal portrait of Princess Diana and her boys, Linda Evangelista from the cover of Liz Tilberis's first issue of the new *Harper's Bazaar*. I told Patrick about growing up with

50

a darkroom in our house, taking photography classes all through school, and waiting in line for an hour and a half to meet Richard Avedon at the Whitney. He took me upstairs to see the studio, and on the way up my heart broke when he told me they had been scheduled to shoot Kate Moss for the cover of *Bazaar* that day but had to cancel because of the weather. He then introduced me to his studio manager Wendell, who showed me around while Patrick disappeared back downstairs. Wendell said he felt bad that I had schlepped all the way down to the studio in a blizzard just to have it be closed, and he asked me if I would like to be an intern for the summer. Without revisiting the idea of Vermont for even a second, I said yes. My whole life changed in that moment.

A year later, in the winter of 1995, we were actually in St. Barts photographing Kate Moss for *Bazaar*. At this point I had been on shoots with Kate a few times, and I was pretty enamored of her, but the only thing she'd ever really said to me was that she loved an antique jade-and-gold ring that I wore, a hand-me-down from my mother. We arrived on set that first day in St. Barts, business as usual, and as I was walking into the kitchen, I heard *his* voice. It was Johnny Depp's. Holy. Shit.

I was that girl who had pictures of Johnny Depp from *21 Jump Street* plastered on the ceiling above her bed. When I was a teenager, his was the last face I saw before I fell asleep every night and the first one I woke up to in the morning. I had at least fifteen different fantasies about how I was going to get Johnny Depp to be my boyfriend. I even wrote him an impassioned letter that I was sure sounded different, more sincere, than all the other fan mail he'd received. Not surprisingly, I never heard back.

Obviously, I knew that he was Kate's boyfriend, but I'd never imagined that he would come to a shoot. I was so stunned that I did a 180 and walked in the other direction. What could I possibly say to Johnny Depp? I avoided him entirely. An hour or so later, I saw him and Kate snuggling in a hammock while we finished setting up the lights. Later that day, they were making out next to

51

the pool. While Kate was being photographed, Johnny lingered around but never got close enough to me to warrant an introduction. I was nervous the whole time—pretty miserable, in fact. How could I be in such close proximity to Johnny Depp and not have the nerve to at least say hello to him?

At the end of shooting, Patrick announced that we would all have dinner at his house that night. I thought for sure Kate and Johnny would stay cuddled up in their room, but they joined us. In fact, I met Johnny minutes after I arrived at Patrick's house. If nothing else happened, at least I'd shaken his hand. But then he sat right across from me at dinner!

Johnny Depp and Kate Moss, each looking as cool as the other, in the late nineties.

We made a little small talk here and there, and our conversations with others crossed paths a few times. But it was pretty obvious that, for him, Kate was the only person in the room. He stared at her the whole dinner. They interlocked their feet under the table. There was an incredibly intense love going on between them.

By the next morning, Johnny had jetted off somewhere, and the shoot with Kate resumed as usual. I never had the same feelings for Johnny Depp again. I was so convinced of his love for Kate that

it seemed time for me to move on. When I look back at pictures of them now, what I notice most is just how good they looked together—their beauty, their clothes, their style, their body language. It's almost too much cool to handle. I guess it was for them, too.

Every single day on set with Patrick was exciting. The list of awe-inspiring shoots went on and on: Janet Jackson's album cover, Nadja Auermann in couture in the Tuileries, Cindy Crawford for the cover of *Bazaar*, Claudia Schiffer (naked!) on the beach in St. Barts, Stephanie Seymour for Victoria's Secret, Bond Girl Carole Bouquet for Chanel N°5. But the highlight for me—hands-down—was Madonna. Patrick was scheduled to shoot the cover for her *Bedtime Stories* album in Miami. I wasn't sure I'd be included; I was just the intern and I assumed Wendell, Patrick's studio manager, would take Christine and Margaret, the first two assistants. But Wendell was a sweetheart—sometimes—and he walked into the studio one day and said, "Well, it's going to be an all-girls trip to Miami next week."

"Really?" I asked in disbelief. I'd been a lifelong Madonna fan—as a teenager I'd dressed up as her for Halloween, for talent shows, sometimes just when I was bored on a Saturday.

"Yup. I'm sending the three of you. I've already worked with Madonna and I have tons to catch up on in the studio. You three will be fine on your own."

"Okay," I said, trying to contain my excitement. "Thank you."

"Don't fuck it up," he said with a wink, and then turned around to leave the room.

It was August in Miami and seriously hot. Christine, Margaret, and I were staying in a small art deco hotel on Collins Avenue. A van came to pick us up at the crack of dawn to take us to the Eden Roc hotel where the shoot would start.

We were there for hours before Madonna arrived. When she finally did, I couldn't believe how *tiny* she was. And that was with six-inch wedge heels on! She wore all black, with black sunglasses and platinum-blond hair that was still wet from the shower. She had a diamond stud pierced through her nose, and I did everything

53

I could not to wince when I caught sight of it. For some reason it looked painful. She was polite and friendly and went around the room introducing herself to everyone on set.

After another couple of hours of hair, makeup, and wardrobe, she walked onto the set wearing nothing more than a fluffy whisp of lingerie. She crawled on the bed in the hotel room and began to work her come-hither moves for Patrick's camera. The whole scene was surreal.

In these situations, I felt invisible. As the intern, barely into my twenties, I was easily the least important person in the room. Sometimes the talent chatted with Patrick's first assistant while they adjusted the camera or took the light reading, but as the third in line I was used to feeling lucky if I even got so much as an introduction. There were some exceptions. I remember Cindy Crawford being incredibly friendly; we once happened to ride the elevator up to the studio together and when I pushed the button for Patrick's floor, she asked me if I was working on the shoot and then introduced herself. "Hi, I'm Cindy," she said, as if I didn't already know. She touched the Elsa Peretti for Tiffany single-diamond necklace on her neck while looking at mine and said, "We have the same necklace."

"Oh, yeah," I replied. "My boyfriend when I was eighteen gave it to me. He said he wanted to be the first man to ever give me a diamond."

"How sweet!" she said.

Another time, on the way home from a shoot in St. Barts, Stephanie Seymour tried to use her miles to upgrade me so we could sit together on the plane. The airline wouldn't allow it, but I was touched by the thought nonetheless. Despite my place at the bottom of the totem pole, I always tried to remember how lucky I was to be even the least important person on any of Patrick's shoots.

After shooting a few rolls of film, Patrick suggested to Madonna that they try a few shots without the nose ring. What a process that was! First her assistant had to call the "nose ring changer," and we waited for a half hour for her to arrive. The "changer" finally arrived and began the complicated process of removing Madonna's nose ring. I guess retouching wasn't the option it is today.

Later on, the whole production moved on to a studio set in South Beach. While posing, Madonna played us her new album and sang along to it. I was *dying*. "*Mmm mmm, something's coming over, mmm mmm, something's coming over me, my baby's got a secret...*" At one point, Ingrid Casares showed up. She was famous for running the nightlife of South Beach, but, more than that, for being Madonna's best friend. She instantly started flirting with Christine, Patrick's first assistant, who happened to like girls.

At the end of the shoot, Madonna thanked us and invited us all to her birthday party that night. It was her thirty-fifth, and she was having a smallish party at her home. Before I got too excited, I remembered that Patrick, Christine, and Margaret were all due to fly back to New York that night. Because I was headed off on vacation straight from Miami, I would be taking a flight out the next morning. However, I knew I wasn't in a million years going to turn up at Madonna's birthday party on my own. As exciting as it sounded, I quickly resigned myself to not going. Later, as I was chilling out in my room after the shoot, the phone rang. It was Patrick. Madonna had convinced him to stay an extra night to go to her party, and he invited me to tag along with him.

I ran out of my hotel and went on a frantic mad dash around South Beach to find something to wear. This was no doubt the most exciting party I had ever been invited to and I had *nothing* to wear! I couldn't even come close to affording anything in the designer boutiques, and the only other options were the more touristy shops along Collins Avenue. All I could find there were cheap Versace knockoffs—midriff-baring stretchy pastel mini dresses made of polyester with plastic-y hardware. Not my look.

In the end I wore my own floral slip dress from good old Contempo Casuals. I usually wore it with a T-shirt underneath (remember that floral-grunge look?), but it was so hot that I wore it on its own. I carried a black braided leather bag I had splurged on at Barneys CO-OP and wore the only shoes I had with me, flat black-and-white leather Jack Rogers sandals. My outfit was pretty, but I didn't feel remotely cool. That moment has stayed with me

throughout my life. I never travel anywhere—*anywhere!*—without being prepared for an impromptu fabulous night out.

Patrick and I arrived at the party on the early side, and there weren't many people there yet. Madonna came right over to us, hugged Patrick, grabbed my hand, and led me around. She took me to the bar, got me a mojito, introduced me to all the other people at the party, and then sat me down next to Gloria Estefan, saying that Gloria would take good care of me. Gloria couldn't have been nicer. She treated me as if I was as important as anyone else in the room and engaged me in conversation. There were probably forty people at the party and I didn't recognize many of them, the majority being Madonna's tour dancers and members of her staff, but Gianni and Donatella Versace were there, as well as Dennis Rodman and Mickey Rourke. The feeling of the party was cozy and friendly and I was having a good time, so much so that I lost track of Patrick and had to navigate my own way through the rest of the evening. When I got up to help myself to the buffet, I saw Fabien Baron, the art director who had been on set that day. He also designed Madonna's *Sex* book and is arguably the most well-known art director in the fashion industry, even today. His assistant Patrick Li was there with him. He was my age and we'd seen each other on shoots together a few times before. We were thrilled to see each other and hung out the rest of the night. The party got wild after dinner, with drag queens showing up on the dance floor and Madonna and all her backup dancers going crazy, dancing, making out. It was a scene I'll never forget.

At one point Patrick came over to check on me, and I told him I was ready to go back to my hotel. It had been a *long* day and I had an early flight in the morning. He wanted to stay longer, so he said he'd try to find me a ride. Minutes later, he returned and told me to get in the car waiting in front of the house. The driver was standing outside and ushered me into the back of a huge white stretch limo. As I crawled in, I caught sight of Gianni and Donatella Versace lounging in the back waiting for me! After the butterflies in my stomach settled down, we chatted all the way back

to South Beach. Just like Gloria, they asked me all about where I was from, what I was studying in college, how the shoot went that day, and what I wanted to be when I was finished with school. We talked about Palm Beach, and they wanted to know what it was like in the seventies when I was a child growing up there.

Twenty years later, the fact that this evening ever happened seems completely surreal. What did stay with me, though, was that the whole night signified for me the best kind of success—it was an example of how being well-known and successful also comes with the responsibility to set a precedent of kindness and generosity for those who look up to you.

As I continued working for Patrick, I was promoted from intern to assistant. The idea that I would now be paid *and* continue on in this dream job seemed too good to be true. It also motivated me to work longer hours, and more often. During my summer break from Brown, I would work for a ten-week spell, and then I would go back for an additional three weeks in January during my extended winter break from college. Occasionally I would even fly

At Madonna's birthday party, I told Patrick Demarchelier I was a fan of Mickey Rourke in Diner, *so he made me pose with him for a picture. I was so embarrassed.*

*Acting as the stand-in
on set in Patrick's studio,
1994.*

over to Paris for fashion week in October during the five-day break
we had for Columbus Day weekend. Patrick's manager was very
supportive about things like that—he wanted me to make the most
of my extracurricular learning and was always happy to slot me in
for work time when I was out of school. We worked in Paris a lot,
but my favorite time to be working there was during the fashion
shows—there was the couture in January and July and the ready-
to-wear shows in October (I could never find time off from school
to go to the February shows).

During the couture shows, our shooting days were *insane*! We'd
report to work at seven A.M. to shoot, say, a Chanel N°5 ad with
former Bond Girl Carole Bouquet in the Hotel Georges V. By late
morning we'd be shooting a cover portrait of, say, Nadja Auermann
for *Bazaar* in a studio in Montparnasse. In the afternoon, Patrick
would go to a few shows—Dior, Chanel, Valentino. Every now and
then he would throw me a bone and get me a press pass through

Bazaar, gaining me admission to the photographer's pit. There I would stand with my simple Pentax K1000 and get elbowed and bullied by the guys actually doing this for a living while I managed to get a few shots of the girls on the runway. There was no digital film then and you wouldn't believe the pushing and shoving that went on when these guys had to change their film at lightning speed. A photographer would bend down, having dropped his film case, and bump into someone else, who would shove back harder while swearing at the first guy in French. I would emerge from the pit sweating and shaking, but completely high from the experience. How many girls can say that the very first fashion show they ever attended was the Chanel Haute Couture show at the Carrousel du Louvre in Paris? Where is there to go from that point, really? Well, I did have places I wanted to go.

My workday wasn't finished there. In the evening, after the shows, we'd be shooting, for example, the couture on Nadja for a *Bazaar* editorial story to go along with her cover shot. Shooting couture is mayhem. There is only one sample of each dress and everyone wants to photograph it. If you want to shoot couture hot off the presses, you have to shoot it in Paris where the fashion houses can be in control of their own samples and where the samples could be available within an hour's notice, should a client be interested in buying a piece. You may get the dress for an afternoon or you may get it for just two hours. We'd be shooting in the Bois de Boulogne or in the Tuileries or in the middle of the Place de la Concorde or in a booth at La Coupole, and there would be men on motorbikes coming and going with a $50,000 dress every hour or so. We'd finish shooting at three A.M. I'd take

One day Patrick wanted to take pictures around Versailles outside of Paris, and I was tasked with rowing him around in a tiny rowboat, which I was nervous was going to tip over. He took this Polaroid of me, 1995.

the film back to my hotel, count and label it all, and prepare it to be picked up first thing in the morning by a special FedEx courier. I'd crash into my bed at four A.M. I'd then get up at seven the next morning and do it all again. I loved every single second of those weeks in Paris, despite the long hours and the grueling, often physical work. The diversity of tasks, the adrenaline, the teamwork, the exposure to a whole new world of people and ideas and talents, every single minute of it excited me. Some friends thought I was crazy to spend my school holidays working, but for me this sure beat an extra few weeks hanging around at home.

While I did and do and always will love photography, my heart had already begun to yearn for more interaction with the clothes we were shooting. On set, when I was done setting up the lights and loading the cameras, I used to help Tonne Goodman's assistant Beau with the unpacking and steaming of the clothes. Tonne was then the fashion director of *Bazaar*, and they would bring trunks and trunks of the most beautiful clothes I'd ever seen along with them on shoots. I couldn't get over the luxury of them—the beading, the fur, the embroidery, the precise tailoring. I had never seen clothes like that up close, and I was mesmerized. They were like magnets to me, attracting all my attention. I just wanted to be near them. I wanted to touch them, make outfits from them, try them on. So when I went to those few shows in the shoes of a budding young photographer, the place I really wanted to be was the front row, right up next to the clothes, choosing what I would buy, what I would shoot, what I would wear. I fantasized about the day when I had earned a place at a fashion show in my own right, with an invitation and a place card that had my name on it.

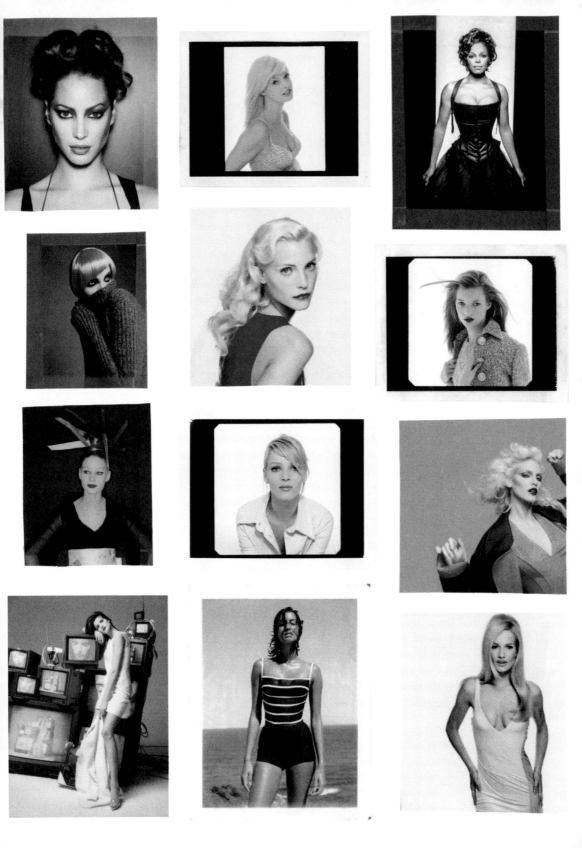

WHILE I AM not inspired by Palm Beach in the typical way—I now refuse to wear Stubbs & Wootton loafers, Belgian Shoes, Jack Rogers's Navajo sandals, or anything by Lilly Pulitzer—the Palm Beach aesthetic is still very much a part of my identity. My Palm Beach, however, is the one that I experienced while growing up there—first year-round and then in the summers—throughout the seventies and eighties. I remember my mother first and foremost in her Lilly sheaths, but also barefoot in her cutoff jean shorts, white cotton

...amisole, ladies gold Rolex, and over-size sunglasses. I remember my dad's friend Countess Tauni de Lesseps in her cable-knit sweater from Trillion with a slim leather belt around her waist and pressed trousers, all in the same pastel shade. One day it was lavender, the next it was yellow, and then pale pink after that. I remember my mom's friend Emilia Fanjul in designer duds from New York, impressing all of us with her perfect grooming and high-style outfits. I remember Anky Johnson in her linen caftan and matching turban—again in a different color each day. I remember Mimi Kemble in her pink-and-black polka-dotted and ruffled one-shoulder bathing suit with impossibly golden blond hair falling halfway down her back. And I remember Susie Phipps Cochran bucking all convention in her army jacket, driving around the largest privately owned property in Palm Beach in a beat-up U.S. Postal Service jeep with the doors missing. Every time I get dressed, the eccentric, highly personal style of the women I grew up around comes to mind and influences the way I see myself.

I am also influenced, albeit somewhat reluctantly, by my grandmother Tonsi's love of matching. Not only did she take her own coordinating to extremes—say, a pink and green floral

belt—but she also had an obsession with matching my sister, me, and my cousin all in identical outfits. Each time we came to visit her in Gulf Stream, Florida (just a half hour down the A1A from Palm Beach), she would have the outfits all laid out on the bed for us, and we would put them on, take a photo, and then go about our day. If our cousins weren't available, she would recruit our next-door neighbor's daughters to partake in this ritual. I don't know what it was about a matching foursome that excited my grandmother so much, but it's clear that she loved a strongly coordinated aesthetic statement. I myself feel a sometimes overpowering urge to match my bag to my shoes, or my handbag hardware to my belt hardware, and I know this must come from Tonsi. In my life I have worked intentionally hard on overcoming the urge to match and have succeeded to some degree. I mix my jewelry, often having white gold, yellow gold, and silver all on the same arm, and I recently bought a Céline bag with both silver and gold hardware on it. I have also gotten better about not having to match my bag and shoes, as long as those colors are balanced out somewhere else in my outfit. But these are hard-won battles, as the hereditary tendency to have a Palm Beach level of coordination is always

Clockwise from top left: Kim and me with Hope and Katie, all in Lilly Pulitzer, 1977. Kim and me having a pony ride alongside our friend Andres, 1977. Kim and me in matching dresses, 1980. My grandfather Jack in a typical all-matching Palm Beach look, 1974. Kim and me with Margaret and Elizabeth, all in Florence Eisman, 1978.

A LONG WALK IS
THE BEST WAY
TO CLEAR YOUR HEAD

WORKING FOR Patrick Demarchelier was my first experience within the actual fashion industry, yet I wasn't there as a wannabe fashion person—I was there as a wannabe photographer. When I started out, I wanted to be like Patrick. But as my summer internship stretched into three years of on-and-off work throughout college, I found myself less enamored of loading cameras and setting up lights. It was either time to strike out on my own as a photographer or try something new. I thought an obvious next step might be working as a fashion assistant at a magazine, given all the publishing people I had formed relationships with while working for Patrick. But Patrick talked me out of the idea. "No, no, no, no, no," he insisted. "A magazine job is not interesting for you. You should work at an art gallery." Art was Patrick's personal passion, outside of photography. Clearly he knew a lot about the art world, and as I had been an art history major at Brown, he thought it would be a good fit for me.

Opposite: Photographer Johnny Pigozzi took this photo of me (sitting on my friend Tara's lap) at Francesco Clemente's post-show party in 1997.

If you can believe it, the way I secured my first art gallery job was eerily similar to meeting Patrick in the restaurant, but this time it was in a shoe store. I was sitting in French Sole, a store

67

devoted entirely to ballet flats, trying on a new pair to wear to my art gallery interviews, when I saw a gray-haired man pause to look in the window. I was the only person visible inside, as the shopgirl had gone downstairs to fetch my size. After looking in through the window for a moment, the man opened the door and said to me, "Is this store new?"

"Uh, no. It's been here as long as I can remember." At this point, I was pretty sure the man was Larry Gagosian, one of the gallery owners to whom I had sent my résumé just the day before.

"Do you live in the neighborhood?" he asked.

"My parents do. I just graduated from college, so I'm living with them." Before he could say anything else I asked, "Are you Larry Gagosian?"

"Yes," he replied, suddenly looking self-conscious and slightly tentative.

"Oh, wow. I just sent you my résumé yesterday. I'm hoping to work at your gallery."

He invited me to go see him at his office that afternoon. You might be rolling your eyes thinking that he was obviously just trying to pick me up, and maybe he was—I did later find out that he lived on the same block as French Sole!—but I wasn't interested in that. I wanted a job at a gallery, and Gagosian was the best. Any girl looking for a job in the art world would be an idiot to turn down the chance to meet with Larry.

So we sat in his office that afternoon and talked about art. He asked me to name all the artists whose work was displayed in his office. I aced them all—there was a Rodin sculpture and paintings by Jasper Johns, Cy Twombly, Damien Hirst, and Picasso. I told him about my love of photography and my interest in Sally Mann. He told me they had just signed her up to do a show at their L.A. gallery. It all seemed to click, and he offered me a job before the interview was over. The money wasn't enough to live on without my parents' support, so I asked if I could sleep on it. It seems insane now to think that I hedged, but I really wanted financial independence from my parents. At 7:45 the next morning, the phone rang.

"Hello?" I said, slightly suspect of anyone calling that early in the morning.

"Hi, it's Larry. Are you taking the job?"

"Um, I don't know yet. I am having breakfast with my parents this morning to discuss it."

"What do you want? Thirty thousand?"

I still wasn't sure that $30,000 was going to make me financially independent, but it was a big increase from his initial offer, and I knew that most of my friends didn't make that much. I decided that I wanted the job then and there, but something in me instinctively knew to make Larry wait.

"Thank you. That's very generous. I will call you later today."

Of course, I accepted the job and my parents were delighted that I'd managed to get some more money out of him.

In many respects, working at Gagosian Gallery was one of the highlights of my career, though I was only just out of college. As an art history major, there was arguably no more prestigious place to work. I met hero after hero of mine, and I was always hopelessly starstruck. I started out being the assistant to Pippa Cohen, the girl who produced all the shows in all three of Larry's galleries—two in New York and one in L.A.—at the time. Once a show went on the calendar, Pippa would set the wheels in motion to make it all happen. The announcement (gallery-speak for invitation), the press release, the catalogue, the celebratory dinner, even the signage for the gallery walls was orchestrated by Pippa, with my assistance. But as luck would have it, Pippa left her job just as I was getting a handle on the scope of her responsibilities, and I inherited her position. I became the person who would liaise with the artists on most of the details regarding their shows—what typeface to use for the catalogue title, who was on the guest list for the dinner, which art-world luminary gave a quote for the press release, the approval of the color correction for the photograph on the announcement, and which piece would be chosen for the show's ad in the *New York Times*. During my two years there, I planned an exhibition for Francesco Clemente and hung out in

his iconic studio on lower Broadway; stayed with Sally Mann in her Lexington, Virginia, home, eating hamburgers and watercress salad (grown in her garden) and poring over her unpublished photographs; chatted with David Salle about how many triptychs to include in an upcoming show; and got hung up on by the cranky genius Richard Serra countless times.

Most treasured of all, I became friends with Cy Twombly. I first met him in St. Barts; Larry had rented a house near Cy's in St. Barts for two weeks. He asked me to come along to help plan activities and meals for his guests, including his girlfriend and a handful of clients and friends. Cy joined us for most meals, and despite being a bit prickly at first (he once told me I asked too many questions!), I eventually learned how to navigate conversations with him. We sat next to each other quite a bit, and at the end of the two weeks, I could tell he had grown fond of me. A month or so later, Cy invited me down to his house in Lexington, Virginia (yes, the same hometown as Sally Mann's), to take a look at the new sculptures he was working on. He gave me a tour of his town and his alma mater, Washington and Lee, and we had lunch at the Palm Parlour, his local hangout. After I left, I wrote him a thank-you note using watercolors. When he received it, he called me at the gallery and told me that my use of watercolors had inspired him to paint again after making sculptures for quite a while. He rang again a few months later to say that he'd seen me featured in a fashion spread in *Town & Country* magazine, and that he felt proud to know me. In addition to being my favorite artist of the twentieth century, Cy Twombly was a lovely man, and I feel so lucky to have known him.

Despite this enviable position in the art world at such a young age, many people who knew Larry Gagosian and the gallery's reputation wondered how I could work there at all, especially as a young person right out of college. The gallery atmosphere was intense and often harsh. The salespeople were ultracompetitive, the artists were vulnerable, and Larry was brilliant verging on crazy. One minute he'd be shouting at me for not correctly intuiting what he

wanted me to do, and the next minute he'd be begging—*begging*—me to take over his East Hampton guesthouse for the weekend with my boyfriend Christopher and as many friends as I liked so he wouldn't have to be alone.

And his *whole* life was work. On Saturdays, when I was working in the city and he was in the Hamptons wondering what to do with himself, he'd call the gallery incessantly—over and over and over again—just to check in, five minutes, one minute, or even seconds after he last called. I almost always told him the same thing—that the gallery was quiet and not much was going on other than the usual visitors passing through. Sometimes he would call back so quickly, so manically, that he would get embarrassed and hang up just as I answered. He was a lot to handle.

At first, I thought it was funny. I'd walk into my friend Tara's office (she was Larry's assistant) after he'd shouted a stream of obscenities at me, and we'd just start laughing. I told people, and myself, that I loved working at the gallery and that Larry's behavior didn't bother me. But after a while, it wasn't as funny as it once was, and the highs and lows were more extreme. *I can handle this*, I thought. *I'm strong and tough and I won't let him get to me, try as he may.* Some days when he yelled at me I'd just leave and walk home. After the first time, I came to expect the surprisingly sincere apology from him waiting on my answering machine when I got home. One time he even sent chocolates.

Halfway through my second year, Larry's unpredictable and often aggressive behavior finally began to affect me. I would find myself yelling at cabdrivers, and wake up feeling dread at the prospect of going in to work. I called in sick a few times, but when I'd worn out that excuse, I started making more and more elaborate excuses for why I was coming to work late or not at all. I am ashamed to admit that I once even claimed that my apartment had been broken into as an excuse for not being able to face work. And on the days when I did pluck up the courage to conquer my resistance, it was increasingly hard to come down from the adrenaline high when I got home in the evening. My

Pages 72–73: The sculpture catalogue that Cy Twombly signed for me. It says "Amanda, Very Fondly, Cy," 1998.

71

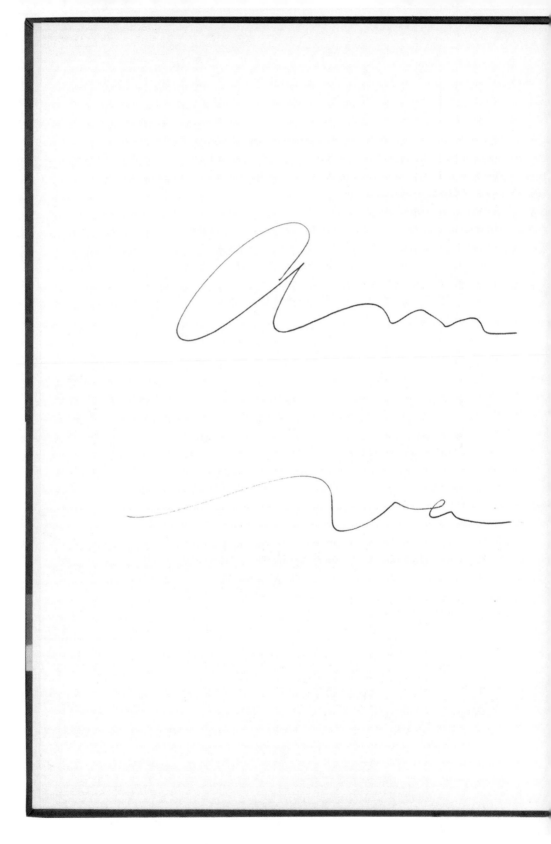

CY TWOMBLY: TEN SCULPTURES

boyfriend Christopher was spending most nights at my apartment, usually coming over around eight, in time for dinner. I really needed that first hour at my apartment alone to calm myself down from the manic energy of the day. Occasionally I would walk home—more than sixty blocks!—to let the stress roll off me so I could arrive home in a more sane state. But one day I took a taxi and Christopher was there early. I'd recently given him keys, and he'd just let himself in. It startled me. I didn't want him to see me in my stressed-out, frenzied state of mind. When I copped to my alarmed reaction, he suggested maybe it was time to move on to another job. My mom was worried, too, and had recently made the same suggestion.

I was pretty sure I didn't want to work in the art world forever. I loved my experience but couldn't see myself as a salesperson, and I didn't love the idea of curating enough to go back to school for it. I thought about going back to fashion, but I didn't even know where to begin. I just wanted a break so badly. My parents were very supportive of my leaving Gagosian, but they had made it very clear that they didn't encourage quitting one job if you didn't have the next one lined up.

Then came a particularly bad day at work. A week earlier, we had gone to print with a Warhol "Dollar Signs" catalogue that was to be shown in Los Angeles. It was my job to do the initial sign-off on the catalogue after thoroughly checking it for errors. Melissa, the director of Gagosian, would give the final sign-off before it went to the printer. Everyone signed their initials, and off it went. The morning after the finished catalogues arrived, we looked through them and everyone was happy. The colors were accurate, the text was clear, and the cover looked beautiful. And then after lunch, I heard Larry storming down the hall toward my office. He slammed the catalogue down on my desk and said, "Fuck you. FUCK YOU, AMANDA!" And stormed out.

I walked down the hall, shakily, to Melissa's office. Melissa was—and still is, all these years later—the head director of Gagosian. She's been Larry's right hand for more than thirty years,

and she is his polar opposite. She is calm, understanding, and laid-back. She was usually the mother hen to all the young women who worked in the gallery, but at this moment, Melissa wasn't happy with me, either.

"Sit down," she said. She pointed to the title page of the catalogue. At the bottom of the page it read GAGOSIAN NEW YORK.

"Yeah . . ." I said, not understanding the problem.

"It should say 'Gagosian Los Angeles.' That's where the show is." Her eyes widened at me in surprise for not noticing it right away.

"But Gagosian is a New York–based gallery," I explained. "I thought all catalogues read 'Gagosian New York' on the title page."

"You should know better. And I will take responsibility for it this time because I signed off on it, too, but if this happens again, there is a line of girls waiting to take over your job."

Of course I was responsible for the mistake and deserved to be reprimanded, but I couldn't get over the "fuck you" that had been shouted at me. I didn't deserve that, and I knew it. If it had happened the year before, I probably would have laughed after he left the room, or defiantly walked out for the day. But now I was just worn down.

Christopher was traveling at the time, so I went to my parents' house that night. I couldn't sleep, not even

in my own bed in my own bedroom. At twenty-three years old, I crawled into bed with my mom and stepfather and finally fell asleep.

The next day, I walked into Larry's office and handed in my notice. "Why?" he asked. I didn't want to pick a fight. I had no fight left in me. I just told him that I was ready to move on. But I did tell Melissa the truth—that I couldn't take the badgering anymore, that the fun, good, inspiring parts of the job were no longer worth the ugly ones. She understood. I'm sure she'd heard the same explanation many times from many girls like me. Or maybe not. But I felt empowered by my choice, like it was the first truly grown-up decision I'd made in my life.

When I left work on my final day, I thought I'd walk home from the gallery on East Seventy-Sixth Street to my apartment on Fourteenth Street. It would be good to clear my head. The next conscious thought I had after that occurred all the way down on Houston Street, nearly a half mile past Fourteenth Street. I kept going. I walked all the way through Tribeca, past the World Trade Center, to Battery Park, at the bottom of Manhattan. Then I turned around and headed all the way back uptown. I wasn't ready to end the peaceful trance the walk had put me in. I ended up back at my parents' apartment on East Sixty-Seventh Street. Yes, I walked nearly eleven miles that night, through the Manhattan streets in the dark, alone. When I arrived, my parents were out for the night, so I just crawled into bed and fell fast asleep.

I don't remember what was going through my head on that walk, just that it gave me a new beginning. I meditated on my freedom long enough to actually physically feel it. So many of the transitional moments in my life have seemed surreal—too foreign to take in at first. My long walk that night—the stress of the job off my shoulders and the opportunity to start again—gave me the chance to absorb it all and wake up the next morning in a new world.

HOW COMMITMENT TO THE MAN OF MY DREAMS SET ME FREE TO BE A FASHION CHAMELEON

IF YOU REALLY WANT to see me light up, you should ask me how I met my husband. It's my favorite question to be asked at a dinner party, and the subsequent conversation, whether it's about the beginning of my relationship or the other person's, always leads somewhere sincere and engaging. In this case, you can't ask me how I met Christopher, but I'm going to tell you anyway, because my marriage to him ultimately provided the solid foundation on which I was able to experiment with careers, personas, lifestyles, friends, and of course fashion.

At age twenty-two I was still in my first year of real life in New York City. Ten months out of college, I lived with my parents on the Upper East Side, worked at Gagosian, went out every night, and somehow managed to wake up early enough to Rollerblade *twice* around the big loop in Central Park every morning. I had made a new best friend at Gagosian. Her name was Tara, and she was truly beautiful—like a cross between Audrey Hepburn and Julia Roberts, with wide doe eyes and a beaming, toothy smile. Most nights after work Tara and I used the money we'd saved from buying a cheap lunch (chicken Caesar salad from the corner deli)

Opposite: In 2000, Christopher and I were on a Vogue *shoot in Montauk. The photographer Arthur Elgort whispered to me that he could tell by our body language that we were going to get married. He took portraits of us and gave them to me as a present when we got engaged months later.*

79

to go across the street to Bemelmans Bar at the Carlyle and have a glass of Sancerre and a bowl of warm nuts, which often substituted for our dinner, before heading off to a gallery opening and then some party downtown that one of our young art-world buddies knew about.

After a few months of doing the "gallerina" social circuit, Tara and I started receiving the occasional last-minute invite from Nadine Johnson, the high-powered publicist in charge of not only Gagosian's best parties but the parties for nearly all the rest of the art and fashion worlds, too. The invites would come at about five P.M., through the fax machine, on the day of. We knew we were only invited when Nadine realized last minute that she needed a few more PYTs at a given party, but we didn't care, we were just thrilled to go. The best last-minute invite we got was for a Versace party in Harlem. They were taking over the once famous Cotton Club to celebrate a new perfume or handbag (I don't remember which), and Donatella herself was the host. Tara and I met up for drinks with Lucy Sykes, a fashion friend from my Demarchelier days (Lucy was Paul Cavaco's assistant at *Bazaar* while I was Patrick's), and we all headed up to Harlem together, wearing our best outfits and our highest heels. I wore my trusty black Joseph pleather pants with a red ostrich feather chubby and vintage red YSL sandals, the latter both from the flea market.

The Cotton Club was packed when we got there, and we pushed our way to the bar to get vodka tonics with two limes. Seeing that the upstairs was less crowded, Lucy and I headed up there, having lost Tara to another friend at the bar. At the top of the second-floor landing, a handsome guy with closely cropped hair and a bleached-out jean jacket caught my eye.

"Who's that?" I asked Lucy.

"That's Looks Brooks!" she responded enthusiastically.

"What?!?" I replied, thinking I'd misheard her over the crowd and the pounding music.

"LOOKS. BROOKS," Lucy repeated. "His name is Christopher, but everyone back home calls him Looks because he was

famous in the eighties for being the best-looking man in England."

I gave Lucy a slightly dubious look, not because he wasn't handsome but because it just seemed like a ridiculous nickname.

"Come, I'll introduce you," she insisted before I had the chance to comment.

But Christopher was engaged in a conversation with someone else, so we stood right behind him pretending to be having our own conversation but really just waiting for him to be free to chat.

"He *is* hot," I mouthed to Lucy behind Christopher's back.

A little tipsy from downing our drinks, Lucy then licked her right index finger and made a *sssssssssizzling* sound while gently touching her finger to his back, making sure he didn't notice. We cracked up.

At the sound of our shrieking, juvenile laughter, Christopher turned around, all calm and sincere and straightforward. He said hi to Lucy and then introduced himself to me. His English accent and his shy smile got to me, even more than his high cheekbones and deep green eyes.

That was it for that night. Not finding much more to say, Lucy and I wandered off to find Tara.

Christopher would later tell me that the Versace party wasn't the first place he'd seen me. He'd spotted me at a Valentine's Day party at the house of a guy I'd been dating, and Christopher had asked a friend who I was, thinking I was cute. The friend explained that I was dating the host of the party, and that was that.

Christopher in all his Looks Brooks glory in Ibiza, 1984.

So a couple of weeks after the Versace shindig, Tara and I were at the afterparty for Juan Uslé's opening at the Robert Miller Gallery. We were with a guy and a girl who decided to dance with each other,

and so Tara beckoned me out onto the dance floor by promising she would teach me to salsa dance. We were at it for hours, laughing as I tried to keep time with her. A couple of drinks into it we found our rhythm and started to look like we kind of knew what we were doing. As we made our way back to the bar on a dance break, I caught Christopher's eye. We waved and smiled at each other but didn't speak that night.

The next day, at Gagosian, the intercom interrupted whatever work I was doing. "Amanda, Christopher Brooks on line one."

"Holy shit," I whispered to myself, and then picked up.

"Hello?" I said, quizzically but not meaning to sound offensive.

After brief formalities, he got right down to it. "You and your friend Tara were so cute dancing last night, and I thought maybe you could set me up with her."

Not skipping a beat, I said, "Sure!" perhaps a bit too enthusiastically. After all, I was already dating someone, albeit casually, and besides, Tara was the prettiest and the nicest girl I knew, and I would be delighted for her to have a superhot boyfriend.

So I invited Christopher to join Tara and me at a friend's dinner party the next night. Tara had a vague idea who Christopher was but was not even a little bit excited by the idea of a blind date. I egged her on and promised she would not be disappointed.

Well, Tara didn't even give herself the chance to be disappointed. She just flat-out ignored him from the minute he got in the cab with us until the minute he left at the end of the night. Nervous from the responsibility of engineering this total failure of a date, I stood talking to Christopher for the majority of the evening. I kept thinking, *God, I'm so American, I can't stop talking!* He even teased me about it.

But then the next day, he called to say thank you for taking such good care of him on an otherwise disastrous evening. By the end of the phone call, he asked *me* out, just as a friend. It seemed innocent enough—we would meet at the MoMA on Saturday to see the Richard Billingham photography show and then have lunch afterward. We had a good laugh that Saturday and said good-bye casually, if ambiguously.

A few days later, he rang again. This time we met for supper at M&R Bar on Elizabeth Street. Over our meal that night he told me that he was still technically married to his first wife, despite having been legally separated for two years. I also asked him how old he was. "Thirty-seven," he replied, both of us silently doing the math and realizing that he was a good fifteen years older than me.

That night I went home, walked into my mother's room, and announced, "I have just had such a nice dinner with the most inappropriate man! He's fifteen years older than me *and* he's separated but still married!" At age twenty-two, no one I hung out with had been married, let alone married and separated. It must have been some subconscious mode of self-protection, because, if I was being honest with myself, I really, really liked him, despite not really being able to accept that I would choose to love someone outside my comfort zone.

Still in denial, we had yet another "friend" date at the movies. We saw *Flirting with Disaster* at Village East on Second Avenue, after sushi at Hasaki on Ninth Street. Christopher reached over and grabbed my hand during the movie. I was surprised, nervous, and completely electrified. Obviously, I don't remember anything else about the movie because my mind and my heart were both reeling.

Afterward, we walked out onto the street. My heart was pounding so hard that I had actually broken out in a sweat. The cool evening air was a huge relief. Before Christopher had a chance to suggest what should happen next, I announced that I would get in a cab and head back uptown. He seemed completely accepting of that. But this time, instead of a polite double kiss on both cheeks, he hugged me. A huge, enveloping, lingering bear hug. We hugged for minutes. It was the best hug I've ever had, before or since. We disentangled, managing not to kiss, and I quickly got myself into a taxi.

Two days later it was my twenty-third birthday, and I decided to cook lamb curry for about twenty friends at my parents' apartment. Because Christopher and I were still firmly in "just friends" status, and had been seeing quite a lot of each other, it would have been weird not to invite him, or so I told myself.

Pages 84–85: Christopher and me heading out to go camping in the Adirondacks, late 1990s.

83

Christopher came to the party, and the guy I had been dating was also there, and the whole effect was dizzying. It's easy to look back now and recognize that I had already clearly moved on, but at the time a single, young guy with a good job and an untethered past seemed like the far more sensible option. Shortly after dinner, Christopher came into the kitchen while I was alone and announced to me that he was heading out. When I offered to walk him out, he interrupted me and said, "I'll say good-bye to you here." At that moment he grabbed my face with both hands and kissed me on the lips, and then he turned and walked out. It was the single most attractive thing any guy has ever done to me.

A few days later, Christopher made a plan for us to have dinner at a Japanese restaurant on Houston Street, but this time he suggested we meet at his apartment just around the corner beforehand. The second I walked in the door, our hello kiss turned into a romantic kiss, and we kissed for three hours on the couch while listening to Everything But The Girl on his stereo. I can't tell for sure why it didn't go further than that, but I'm glad it didn't. The kissing was intense. It was enough. We walked out to eat dinner and couldn't make it down one block without stopping to kiss some more. After dinner, he asked me to stay the night, and I declined, shying away from the idea of getting undressed in front of him so soon. Besides, I was fulfilled on every level, having waited so long to find the right moment to let things turn romantic with Christopher and to begin to trust him.

The next day, Christopher rang me at the office, asking if we could get together to talk before meeting up with some friends that night. "Sure," I replied.

After work, I met Christopher in SoHo next to the N/R subway station on Prince Street. We walked a few blocks and then sat down on the stoop of a building where it was quiet.

"Listen," he started. "I've been having a great time with you, but I don't think I'm ready for a girlfriend yet." I was surprised, and I instantly felt vulnerable. I wasn't even thinking that far ahead yet, but who wants to date someone who doesn't want anything

more than that? Somehow I managed to wrap myself in instant self-protection and say, "Yeah, I don't think I'm ready for that either." We agreed to go our separate ways after that night and take a break from seeing each other. I was disappointed, but relieved to have seen the situation through relatively unscathed.

Except he called at eight o'clock the next morning. Thankfully, I was out for a run. He left a message on my answering machine saying that he missed me. *What kind of break is that?* I thought. I don't know how I had the strength to not return his call, but I do know that I have a healthy instinct for self-preservation and if he was telling me that he didn't want a girlfriend, I was going to believe him and not keep walking down that road. At other times in my life I may have been less willing to leave it all behind, but I was coming off the only two years since my mid-teens that I hadn't had a steady boyfriend. Until then I had been a serial monogamist—I had had a consecutive series of yearlong relationships over the past five years. After my sophomore year in college I decided I needed to take myself more seriously, so I left boys behind and became very dedicated to doing well in school and gaining independence on my own. Following some recent dating and one brief relationship, I now felt ready to have a boyfriend again, but I was out of practice and feeling particularly vulnerable.

Two days later a package arrived for me at my parents' house. It was the Everything But The Girl cassette tape that Christopher and I had listened to while making out at his apartment. I still didn't respond, but I can't say I wasn't excited by the attention.

The next week, I forced myself to go out in the evening, having called it off with both Christopher and the other guy I'd been dating. I headed down to Wall Street to see a big art fair that my visual arts teacher from Brown was participating in. There was a long line to get in. While standing there on my own, there was a tap on my shoulder. It was Christopher. On freaking Wall Street, of all random places to be! We chatted, both feeling a bit shy with each other, and he said he'd like to see me again. I knew he was headed back to England in a few weeks' time for most of the summer, so I

87

asked him what the point of that would be. It wasn't that I didn't want to—I was *dying* to. But I was untrusting now. He had turned me down once, and it hadn't felt good. In fact, it felt awful. But I was grateful to have that shock in the early days before I'd really put my heart on the line. "Well, when I'm back in the autumn, it would be great to see you. But I'll let you call me."

"I'm not going to call you" was the last thing I said to him.

The very next night, Nadine Johnson rang and asked me to supper at her house. This was a whole new level of friendship for us, and I was flattered.

You won't believe who Nadine sat me next to.

Yes.

Christopher.

I had no idea that Christopher knew Nadine, and she had no idea that we knew each other.

Chalking the whole evening up to fate, we went out to the garden after dinner and kissed. Then we kissed some more in the bathroom. Then we went home together and never looked back. I went to Europe three weeks later to spend my summer vacation with him. We went to his friend's wedding together in Paris and then came back to England to spend a week on the farm where he grew up.

That was eighteen years ago.

Our road to dating and then living together and then marriage and then children was bumpy. Really bumpy, at times. It took quite a few sessions with a relationship therapist and a life coach to get us to where we are in our marriage today, but here we are.

The reason I am telling you this is because it was, and is, the most important thing that happened in my life. Creating and maintaining a life with Christopher can be very challenging at times, but it is the thing I care most about in the whole world. If nothing else happened in my life, I would feel accomplished simply for the family, the love, the support we have created together. This sense of place I found at a young age gave me a base, a foundation, a sense of security from which to figure out the rest of my life.

Coco, Zach, Christopher, and me posing for the J.Crew catalogue, 2009.

I have changed direction many times in my career. I have worked for big corporate companies and little tiny start-ups, I have earned impressive salaries and also traded work for clothes, I have taken risks and encountered failure, I have reinvented myself through clothes again and again. If I had allowed my career or my clothes to truly define me, I think I would have gotten lost along the way. And actually I *have* gotten lost a handful of times. But I haven't lost myself, because I always have the same person who loves me despite those experiences to return home to and to remind me of who I truly am.

CHRISTIAN LOUBOUTIN

Christian and me drinking champagne on the dance floor at Natasha Fraser's wedding in Paris, 1997.

I WAS twenty-three when I met Christian, and I remember it was the first time as an adult that I felt glamorous. Having worked for Patrick Demarchelier on and off for three years, I had been exposed to many fabulous people and places, but I never associated them with myself. In those days, my body was pretty shapeless, I was always dressed like a tomboy in Levi's, a tank top, and Converse All-Stars, and I spent most of my time hauling studio lights and loading cameras. I was also growing out my drastic Jean Seberg haircut.

After only a week of dating Christopher, he invited me to go to a wedding with him in Paris. *Why not?* I told myself. Only issue? What to wear. I packed a gray bias-cut slip dress from Zara to go with a feather-covered Jamin Puech bag I had bought on a whim in Paris a few months before. The only thing missing was shoes to wear with the outfit, but since we had a few days in Paris before the wedding, I thought it'd be a fun excuse to go shopping.

No such luck. It was the night before the wedding and I still hadn't found the right shoes. We went to the rehearsal dinner at a trendy restaurant called Natacha. I was intimidated because I didn't think I would know a soul there. I hardly even knew my boyfriend! After a lap around the room, I ran into my friend Olga, who I knew because her boyfriend had gone to Brown with me. Instant relief. She came and sat with us, and intro-

duced me to lots of her friends. When I told her about my shoe dilemma, she pointed across the room at a guy in a yellow-and-purple-checked shirt and said that he had the best shoe shop in Paris. She would take me there the next morning.

Four hundred and fifty dollars for a pair of shoes?!?!? I'd never seen such a thing. But I loved them, they went perfectly with my dress, and I was in real trouble without them, so I swallowed hard and put down my credit card. They were strappy burgundy silk stiletto sandals with a small gold ring around the skinny heel. I wish I still had them now to show you.

I arrived at the party that night wearing my new Louboutin shoes, and Christian himself was the first person at the party to come speak to me. He was funny and engaging and incredibly friendly. We later found each other on the dance floor and pretty much stayed there for the rest of the night.

My second pair of Louboutins were much more easily acquired, at least with regard to money if not time. A few months after meeting Christian, I was back in my office at Gagosian when he called and instructed me to look out the window toward Madison Avenue. He explained that he was staying across the street at the Carlyle—in Diane von Furstenberg's apartment—and he won-

dered if we could see each other from the windows. We giggled as we tried to spot each other, to no avail. So instead we made a plan that I would go over to visit him on my lunch break that day.

When I arrived at DVF's apartment (feeling right at home, having spent time there when I dated her son, Alex), my heart leapt as I got a glimpse of the entire living room floor covered in shoes! Christian was holding his market appointments with all the big department stores—Saks, Neiman, Barneys—there over the next few days, and he had all the best pairs from his new collection lined up in perfect rows. I loved feeling that I was among the very first people to see all these amazing designs, before the rest of the world—the editors, the buyers, and the customers. In retrospect, I realize that might have been the first time I felt the behind-the-scenes rush of new fashion bursting forth into the world—surely an omen of things to come just a few years down the road in my career.

"Go ahead! Try them on!" Christian insisted.

I happened to be the sample size, and each pair fit perfectly. Red satin dominatrix sandals, black suede pumps with just the right toe cleavage, soft leather flats with perfect roundness in the toe, evening stilettos with a dramatic bow draped diagonally over the foot. I must

have been lost in thought or overcome by lust, because I remember Christian's voice piercing the silence when he announced, "I have a thought! Why don't you be my shoe model this week? Come over on your lunch break and try on all the shoes for the stores." I couldn't think of anything more exciting.

The next day and the two that followed, I snuck out of Gagosian at lunchtime, headed over to Christian's impromptu showroom in the Carlyle, and walked back and forth across DVF's living room showing off the most beautiful shoes I had ever seen, let alone worn. It was heaven. And I felt so lucky.

After the last appointment, I kissed Christian good-bye and on the way out the door he handed me the sample pair of the red satin dominatrix sandals—a gladiator-inspired stiletto way before gladiator shoes were ever cool—as a gift for my time. I still have those shoes, and I was so proud to wear them fifteen years later when we celebrated Christian's book launch at Barneys.

Four years after my shoe modeling days, I married Christopher, and Christian made my wedding shoes (and my bridesmaids') as a present. When asked by the *New York Times* how we met, here's how he replied:

Mr. Louboutin said it was appropriate he was celebrating Ms. Cutter's wedding, since their friendship began at a wedding years ago. "I was so impressed because she was the only woman I didn't know at the wedding, and I know everybody," he said, "but also because she could dance and dance in these gorgeous six-inch heels as if they were sneakers." He paused. "Of course, they were my shoes, so that was also a great source of pleasure."

ON THAT same first trip to Paris with Christopher, he took me to Brasserie Lipp to have dinner with an old friend from England. I thought it would be a pretty chill dinner and made no effort to look "fashionable." As we walked in, the first person who caught my eye was a woman in a perfectly tailored suit, with cleavage on full display and a veil covering her face. I had no idea who she was and I had never seen a woman dressed so meticulously, so dramatically. Where I came from, style was more discreet, more innate, and this woman drew my attention.

As soon as she saw us, Issy jumped up and shouted, "Looks Brooks!" using that same nickname left over from Christopher's teenage heartthrob years. I was intimidated by the situation and embarrassed by my boring outfit, and I assumed this exotic creature would talk about herself the whole evening.

I was wrong. Issy was warm and engaging and wanted to know everything about me. Her enthusiasm for creativity and talent was apparent from the first moment we spoke. When I mentioned that I had been a photography major in school, she insisted I send her pictures from my portfolio. (When I did, weeks later, she immediately called me and encouraged me to pursue photography as a career.) Later that evening, Issy asked us if we'd seen

Alexander McQueen's Givenchy show. When we said we hadn't, she insisted on walking us through the showroom herself that very night! The way she talked about clothes with such knowledge and passion confirmed to me that clothes were more than just pieces of cloth you put on your body. Clothes had deep social, emotional, cultural, and personal meaning to Issy, and I felt compelled to listen carefully. From Issy I learned to feel empowered, not shy, when making a big fashion statement, as I would grow more comfortable in doing in the following years.

I saw Issy a dozen more times over the years, and she always asked me if I had quit my day job to become a photographer. I never did, but I still tote my camera wherever I go, and she was always one of my most willing subjects.

Opposite: I took this photo of Issy at a dive bar in Paris, 1999.
Above: Dinner with Issy (and her hat!) and Aeneas MacKay at Cipriani Downtown, 2000. Photo by me!

TAKE THE THING YOU MOST LOVE TO DO ON WEEKENDS AND TURN THAT INTO YOUR CAREER

GROWING UP, my older sister, Kimberly, was the one who loved fashion. She was the one with the eighties Fashion Plates toy that enabled you to make outfits for the girl of your choice and then fill them in with patterns using colored pencils. She was the one dragging me to the mall to shop at The Limited and Benetton, and once she even dyed and permed her hair to look more like Molly Ringwald in *The Breakfast Club.*

While Kim was busy loving fashion and style, I was at gymnastics class or on a skateboard with my best friend Alexandra, or, even more precariously, lying down in the middle of the street to act as a hurdle for the boys to jump over on their BMX bikes. I often look back at that time and ask myself how I got from being a complete tomboy to here. When did I fall in love with fashion?

In high school, I dated a boy named Robby, whose stepmother was fashion designer Carolyne Roehm. She looked completely immaculate at all times, even when wearing jeans on the weekend. The only thing I related to about the way she dressed were the Goody faux-tortoiseshell barrettes in her hair. Everything else she wore was silk, cashmere, or fur, and it all matched and was

Opposite: With my friend Leah Forester, playing dress-up in the vintage clothing shop she once owned.

97

perfectly pressed. Feeling the need to look more polished while spending weekends and holidays at their home, I bought my first real designer clothes—a pair of Gucci lizardskin loafers, 80 percent off at the outlet store in Secaucus, New Jersey, and red Ralph Lauren jodhpurs I found on sale at the Eastchester branch of Lord & Taylor.

Another influence in high school was my irreverent friend Samantha Phipps. Her background was as privileged, WASPy, and "tasteful" as they come, but she didn't want to be defined by that. Yes, she wore the requisite Laura Ashley floral-print dresses that all our friends had at the time, but she wore hers with fluorescent orange cowboy boots. She also had long, painted red nails (at age fifteen), and she was the first of my friends to get a tattoo. Sam's unique spirit taught me the importance of being myself and that the first step to self-discovery, in style as in all else, happens by not always following the rules.

Although I can look back now and see the first rumblings of my fashion evolution in high school, I wasn't consciously aware of the role clothes could play in my life until I arrived at Brown. When I first got there I made friends from similar backgrounds and with similar attitudes. While I was comforted by the familiarity, I longed to experience something new. It didn't take me long to find it. My roommate Christy was British, and her older sister Suze hung out with a very cool and certainly more sophisticated gang of friends, most of them from Europe or New York City. I was intrigued but also intimidated. Their clothes were carefully considered, their hair perfectly colored, their nails immaculately manicured. They were exquisite, exotic creatures. Christy was more au naturel, like me, and together we set about trying to glam ourselves up, not so much to impress the older girls but because we were inspired by them (well, maybe a bit of both).

Soon Christy and I were having weekly manicures (I know, a ridiculous thing to do in college), trolling the mall for the trendiest clothes we could afford (yet again, thank God for Contempo Casuals), and obsessively reading every monthly fashion magazine we

could afford. Despite all this, working at Demarchelier brought me back to my tomboy roots—as a photographer's assistant, I needed to be practical, and it wasn't my place to stand out for what I wore. But at Gagosian, I was expected to look current and fashionable, and I enjoyed pursuing my fashion ambitions once again.

Shortly after I left Gagosian, I was having dinner with my friend Harlan Peltz, who asked me what I wanted to do next. I wasn't sure. He said, "Well, it's easy. Take the thing you most love to do on weekends and turn that into your career." Without thinking too long, I realized what I most liked to do was go to the flea market and buy vintage handbags. I figured that in my collection of bags there were a whole lot of design ideas one could use to make new bags. Take the shape from one, combine it with the material of another, and add the hardware of yet another. And so I decided that I'd become a handbag designer, despite having no related experience. I compiled an old linen album with photos, drawings, tear sheets, and collected inspirations that exemplified my style. Then I loaded up an old suitcase with all my vintage bags and called everyone I knew who might introduce me to potential employers.

I got two results. My girlfriend Plum Sykes, who was (and still is) a fashion writer at *Vogue*, recommended the hairdresser Frédéric Fekkai. The majority of his company had just been bought by Chanel, and they had plans to turn it into a full lifestyle brand, including hair accessories and handbags. They were looking to hire someone to oversee their accessory lines. I hauled my stuff in there and had a great meeting with Frédéric and his deputy Michelle. Even with no experience in designing handbags (or designing anything, for that matter!), through my creative presentation, my enthusiasm, and my recommendations from respected people in the fashion world, I was able to convince him that with the support of a technical designer I was up for the task. The very next day he offered me the job of creative director, accessories, at exactly double the salary of my previous job.

The other interview came about through David Lauren (Ralph's son), whom I'd gotten to know as a teenager when he lived in the

same building as my middle school best friend. After an hour and a half of waiting in the reception room, during which time I got a stomachache from nervously ingesting dozens of handfuls of M&M's from the engraved silver bowl on the table next to me, I was interviewed by Buffy Birrittella, Ralph's famously tough right-hand woman. She was gracious and said she liked my presentation but that the accessories department was in flux, and she made it clear that they would be offering only a junior position to me, if any at all.

Ralph has a legendarily focused and established aesthetic, whereas at Fekkai, I could be in charge of the whole creative tone. So I accepted the job at Fekkai, and at age twenty-four, my entrance to the world of fashion was official.

amélia
from the panier de campagne collection

SHOWN HERE IN WOVEN STRAW WITH GREEN CALF LEATHER TRIM AND STUDS.
ALSO AVAILABLE IN WOVEN STRAW WITH RED OR BLACK CALF LEATHER TRIM AND STUDS.

08

margaux
from the les pom-pom collection

SHOWN HERE IN NATUREL GRANA DI RISO WITH ROSE TRIM.
ALSO AVAILABLE IN NATUREL GRANA DI RISO WITH HERBE GREEN TRIM.

8

danielle and zoé
from the les tulipes collection

SHOWN HERE IN CRÈME/BLEU WITH SILVER AND HERBE GREEN WITH SILVER.
ALSO AVAILABLE IN APRICOT WITH GOLD AND CREME/ROSE WITH BRONZE.

11

tatiana
from the panier velours collection

SHOWN HERE IN MAGLINA STRAW WITH BLUE VELVET TRIM.
ALSO AVAILABLE IN MAGLINA STRAW WITH BLACK OR CORAL VELVET TRIM.

01

Some of the bags that I designed with Bruno Frisoni while I was creative director, accessories at Fekkai. They were inspired by Provence.

FASHION LESSON NO. 3
BELLS AND WHISTLES

WHEN I WAS in my twenties, I had to be strategic about buying clothes that were versatile. If I bought a suit, it was dark gray; if I bought a winter coat, it was black; if I bought a cashmere sweater, it was navy. These big-ticket items had to last me a good while and match with nearly everything in my closet. In order to make my outfits more interesting, however, I started a collection of cheap chic "bells and whistles" as I liked to call them. They were just the odd whimsical item here and there that added something un-expected to my look. These were the things I had the most fun shopping for. I remember walking down rue Vieille du Temple in the Marais in Paris pok-ing my nose into each boutique until I found one that looked affordable and interesting. It was the nineties when those jelly-colored Mac laptops were all the craze and I found a bright green rubber watch that was completely of that moment. I wore it for two years. Also in Paris I combed the flea mar-ket and found vintage military pins, old bangles, silk flowers, and fringed shawls. I also loved wandering the New York flea market. I once found a pair of chunky hoop earrings made from teal sequins that I wore to parties for at least a year. As I learned what worked for me and what didn't, and as I started to earn a little more money, I

became bolder in my choices and made bigger investments in the pieces that added more personality to my style. A burgundy sequin evening bag that I bought for $150 at a Chanel sample sale became a surprising staple that I wore regularly for years on end, although a pair of red suede stiletto boots—they were the most beautiful things you'd ever seen—from the Stephane Ké-lian sample sale only got worn maybe three or four times. They just didn't go with enough in my closet. As I've got-ten older, I still use bells and whistles to add character to my outfits, and as I've gained wisdom about what is "me" and "not me," I've been able to simplify the collection and just have a few key things from the most humble—simple red lipstick often does the trick—to the most indulgent—my Chanel shooting star engagement ring.

Opposite: My sequined Chanel evening bag.

TRACEE ELLIS ROSS

TRACEE WAS my first truly high-fashion friend. We met at Brown when I was a freshman and she was a junior. She was extraordinary looking—big beautiful brown eyes, perfect coffee-colored skin, and a headful of immaculate curls. As Diana Ross's daughter, she had in her closet many incredible designer pieces from her mother's fashion heyday in the seventies. She had Missoni flares, Halston gowns, Giorgio di Sant'Angelo jumpsuits, and countless sky-high platform shoes. You would expect the daughter of such a glamorous pop star to have all these clothes in her possession, but seeing them in the context of college was unexpected and at first quite intimidating. But Tracee never wore her clothes in an ostenta-tious way—she would wear one over-the-top thing with other casual, more down-to-earth pieces mixed in. She was the first high/low dresser I ever encountered. She was also the first girl I met who had a signature scent. It would take me twenty years to find my own signature scent (Molecule 01 by Escentric Molecules), but to this day when I smell L'Artisan Parfumeur's Vanille Absolument, I think of Tracee.

Opposite: At Brown, I became interested in fashion photography and Tracee was a willing subject. I trusted her to put on whatever she felt like, and she always looked amazing.

INFORMATIONAL INTERVIEWS

I would not have made it very far in the fashion industry without the support of the mentors who have helped me find my way from time to time. In an effort to repay that generosity, I have always made a conscious effort to make time to talk with people who are new to fashion and trying to figure out their own path. In New York we call these "informational interviews." It means that while I may not have a job opening to offer you, I am still willing to hear about your dreams and aspirations so that I can recommend you to others or call you if I have a position that opens up. Informational interviews can often be equally or more important than actual job interviews, because these people, if impressed by you, are basically willing to use their powerful contacts to help you make connections you would otherwise never get on your own and can lead to some incredible opportunities. I have helped fashion newcomers get summer internships at Diane von Furstenberg, Barneys, Rag & Bone, and Chanel. I even helped an impressive babysitter who was working as a junior writer at a Christian Science magazine get hired as the assistant to the editor in chief at *Teen Vogue*. She has had a successful career in fashion publishing ever since. Some of these meetings with fashion newcomers have been empowering and uplifting, to them and to me, and culminated in great results, while others have been infuriating and felt like nothing more than a waste of my time.

Here are some suggestions for having a successful "informational interview," or any interview, for that matter. Let's pretend you are meeting with me!

1. Have a goal in mind. I want to be able to help you move forward with your ambitions, but I can't help you know what you want. If you know you want to work in fashion (or in any field), but don't know what area, you need to just choose something more specific and go for it. If you try it and don't like it, then you can cross it off your list and pursue the next option. Sitting still and endlessly pondering your direction will not make your path clearer. I want you to say to me, "I would love to work in publishing," or "I am interesting in exploring the retail side of fashion," or "I am passionate about working for a designer." If you feel you are focused but flexible, then give me two or three areas that you would be excited to pursue, but whatever you do, don't say "I don't know."

2. If you love fashion so much, show me! Tear

106

sheets, collages, scrapbooks, anything. Tell me about the magazines you read, the designers you love, the stores you frequent. When I hired Chelsea, my best intern ever, she stole the job away from someone I was on the brink of hiring because she referenced all the pictures she'd ever seen of me in *Vogue*. Yes, this did massage my ego, but as I was looking for a photo researcher, it showed me that she had a prolific knowledge of fashion imagery and a good memory. Either that, or she was a stalker! Thankfully, she turned out to be the former.

3. Take advantage of my experience and wisdom. Ask me what I have learned in the industry, what I have loved most, hated the most, the jobs that have given me the most satisfaction, etc. I want you to feel you have learned something from me, and I want to know that you are curious, hungry for knowledge and wisdom, and willing to take full advantage of opportunities presented to you.

4. Dress the part. Of course I am going to notice every single thing you are wearing, and I'm going to be analyzing what it says about you. I'm sure that intimidates you, but clothes are the language of this industry, and they will be the first thing that gives me a sense of who you are. So yes, the pressure is on! When in doubt, underplay it instead of overplaying it. You don't have to knock my socks off—I just want to see that you have some sense of taste and style when it comes to clothes. One time I interviewed a girl who had on every piece of designer clothing that she owned—a Burberry plaid scarf, Tory Burch "Reva" flats, a Coach bag, a Kate Spade trench. It was just all too much and showed no inherent personal style. I would be so much more impressed by someone who was wearing something I liked and I *didn't* know who designed it. Zara is a great choice in this regard—on trend, doesn't break the bank, and doesn't scream any one designer, unless you go for the supertrendy pieces . . . best to avoid those. I still remember what Laura Stoloff, my assistant at William Morris Endeavor and Barneys, wore when she first came to my office for her interview: a Phillip Lim black leather jacket with a ruffled hem, a white T-shirt, and a set of pearls. I don't remember the trousers or shoes, just that she looked great all around. The jacket was impressive—a pricier item than I'd expect a twenty-three-year-old to have, but she didn't come off as spoiled or pretentious, so I assumed it was a special treat from her parents or something she saved up for to buy on sale. It showed me she understood that a special classic piece was sometimes worth a splurge. Knowing her now for many, many years, my assumption proved true. She is a girl who buys few things, but when she has the chance, she knows exactly the right piece to pounce on. I am so happy today when I see her picture in the press or on blogs being celebrated for her style. She deserves it.

5. Show me how grateful you are for my time. Fashion professionals are busy people. I would always have some resistance to informational interviews because you never know what you are going to get—someone who inspires me to make a few calls and send a few e-mails after they have left, or someone who makes me feel that I've just lost a precious half hour of my day. If you're great, that is reward enough in itself, but just to be sure, bring me a cookie or a flower or a coffee and send me a really nice thank-you note afterward. Handwritten!!!!!

WHEN A ROCK STAR ASKS FOR YOUR PHONE NUMBER, HE DOESN'T JUST WANT TO BE YOUR FRIEND

BY WONDERFUL coincidence, the first three jobs I had in fashion involved me going to Paris regularly. I *love* Paris. If I ever move to a city again, it's the only one I can imagine living in—walkable, beautiful, and full of inspiration.

When I was twenty-four and working for Frédéric Fekkai, I was often in Paris on my own. Unlike my friends who were there to attend fashion shows, I was there for Première Vision, the biggest fashion fabric trade show in the world. I'd rush to get my orders done in the morning, leaving me plenty of time for shopping and then dinner with friends. One night I met a bunch of girlfriends at Hôtel Costes for dinner. Hôtel Costes is still cool, but back in 1999 it was the coolest place in Paris. My friends Lucy and Plum Sykes had recently been designated "It Girls" by the *New York Times* Style section, so they were able to score us a good table. It was such a fun night—lots of wine, chatting, and flirting with the guys at the next table, who kept sending us drinks.

After midnight, when we were starting to think about going home, the actor Billy Zane approached our table to ask if we wanted to go out dancing with him and some friends. When we failed to

Opposite: Mick Jagger and me at the Hôtel Costes in Paris, 1999. I get embarrassed by the over-excited look on my face every time I see this photo.

109

accept immediately, he discreetly whispered that he was with Mick Jagger. Much less discreetly, we whipped around to look at his table, and there was Mick Jagger, looking right at us. "Come on, girls!" he called out. Needless to say, we jumped out of our chairs.

Mick and co. drove us to a nightclub (I can't remember which one—I was too distracted by the excitement) and ordered a giant bottle of champagne. We all migrated to the dance floor. I remember how self-consciously uncool I felt dancing in my outfit. The previous day I'd received a present from my mom—an invitation to buy myself a pair of nice winter shoes while I was in Paris. (She has always very generously made sure I have a few—but not *too* many—good things to wear.) I went straight to the Louboutin store and settled rather practically on a pair of beautiful black leather boots; they reached all the way up to the knee and had an elegant but weather-friendly *flat* crepe sole. Usually I would have dressed up more to have dinner at a sexy restaurant with my girlfriends, but I was too excited about my new boots not to wear them. It didn't help that I paired them with a puce-colored, crushed velvet, *below-the-knee*, bias-cut skirt and a vintage teal cardigan. So nineties.

I was trying to get the rhythm of dancing in my heavy winter boots when Mick made his way over to me (in his sleek tailored trousers and barely buttoned shirt), grabbed my hips, and started dancing. And I mean *really dancing*. I think I went into some kind of trance, because I barely remember any of it, and I wasn't that drunk. Okay, I was pretty drunk, but the rest of the evening, before and after, is clear enough in my memory. All I know for sure is that I let go and danced like mad. We took a few breaks, all as a group, to go back to our table and get another drink and sit down for a minute. And every time we went back to the dance floor, Mick wanted to dance with me. I am an okay dancer, but not a great one. Like most people, my dancing ability increases in direct proportion to the amount of alcohol I consume. Even in the moment, I realized that I'd never danced better in my whole life. You know what happens when you play tennis with someone who is miles better than you, and you play above your usual ability? Well,

Mick raised my dancing game, and I'm reminded of that night every time I hear "Moves Like Jagger" on the radio. Adam Levine isn't kidding.

Four hours later, we stepped out onto the street. Although we were still in a group, I was nervous. All my friends were obviously wondering if Mick was going to try to take me home. It wasn't possible: As much as I was loving the attention, I'd already been with my future husband, Christopher, for two years. I was deeply in love with him and knew for sure that I'd never do anything to jeopardize that. So when we all piled into Mick's car, I was relieved when he whispered into my ear, "If you give me your number, maybe we can go dancing again some time." I wrote it down for him but thought, *Well, that's nice of him to ask, but he's never going to call.* He gave me a kiss on the cheek. Nice guy. Perfect night.

But then he called! I'd been back at work in New York for a week when the phone rang. The number was blocked, and I didn't dare pick up, thinking it might be *him*. "Hi, uh, Amanda . . . it's Mick," his sleepy voice said on my answering machine. "I'll be in New York next week and I thought we could see each other." (When I would leave that job a year later, I recorded that message, which I'd saved, so that I could keep it as a souvenir of my unlikely encounter. I must still have it somewhere today.)

Here is where the delusion began. I *had* to call him back; it would be too much of a shame not to. And then if he asked to see me, it would be too rude to say no. Saying "Well, I have a boyfriend" on the phone seemed unimaginably awkward and lame. And I did want to see him again—I just didn't want to sleep with him. Or kiss him. Or anything. You must be rolling your eyes. I'm actually rolling my eyes as I write! But I was twenty-four, so give me a break.

I decided that if he'd agree to have lunch with me, I would do it. How dangerous could lunch be? I was so nervous calling him back. I remember that my voice was shaking. We agreed to have lunch the next day—he suggested I meet him in the lobby of the Pierre and then we'd walk to a neighborhood restaurant.

From left: Anh Duong, Lucy Sykes, me, and Plum Sykes on our night out with Mick in Paris, 1999.

Did I really think Mick Jagger and I were going to walk down the street together and casually pop in somewhere to eat? Without having our picture taken? If it crossed my mind at the time, I ignored it. But I knew I had to tell Christopher what I was doing—having lunch with Mick Jagger. Being the annoyingly unflappable person he is, Christopher said, "Say hi to him for me."

So I naively walked into the Pierre looking for Mick. I wore my second-favorite pair of Joseph trousers—mushroom-colored flares with a burgundy velvet tuxedo stripe up the side; a chunky, cream-colored Narciso Rodriguez sweater; and my favorite hunter green suede Stephane Kélian high-heeled boots. My goal was to be stylish but not overtly sexy. When I didn't see him in the lobby, I went up to the desk and gave the secret code name he had instructed me to use. The clerk nodded to a burly, plainclothed man in the corner, who approached me. "Right this way, Miss Cutter," he said, showing me the way to an elevator. When he pressed PH, I began to understand that I was in trouble. How was I going to get out of this?

The man led me off the elevator, through the second door of a foyer into a giant apartment, and then disappeared. Mick was on the sofa, with a small table set for two nearby and Mary J. Blige playing on the stereo. It was *awful*. I was so nervous. I was terrified of sitting down next to him on the couch, but it was clear that lunch wasn't going to be served yet, so I just stood around for a few minutes trying not to look too mortified. We talked about what he was reading in the *New York Times* (something to do with India) and then he suggested I sit down on the sofa. Not wanting to be the idiot who forbids a kiss before he even tries, I sat down tentatively. He suggested I come closer, as if we were definitely more than friends. That's when I looked sheepish and said, "I can't."

"I'm really sorry," I explained. "I had a great time with you in Paris and I thought it would be fun to see you again, but I have a boyfriend who I really love and who you actually know." When I explained that I was with Christopher (who knew Mick through his sister, Annabel), he laughed sweetly and then immediately relaxed, as did I, to a smaller degree. We ate our lunch—a rather banal

spaghetti with tomato sauce and basil—while chatting about the friends we had in common, what we loved about New York, and, oddly enough, about his parents. Over the course of lunch, I began to feel like he was no longer *rock star* Mick Jagger. He was lovely and soft and sweet and, in a weird way, almost protective of me—almost like a father having lunch with his daughter. (I suppose that isn't such an odd idea, considering he is more than thirty years older than I am.) We had a friendly hug good-bye that afternoon.

Much to my surprise, it wasn't the last time I saw Mick. He called me a few weeks later, just to say hi, and when I told him I would be in Paris the next month he suggested we go out dancing again. We did meet up, as before, with his friends and mine, and we had another dance. The energy wasn't as high that night, now that we were definitively just friends, but it was fun nonetheless. We didn't talk again on the phone, but I see him from time to time with mutual friends or at a fashion show. He is always as friendly and sincere as he was that embarrassing day on the couch at the Pierre.

STYLE INFLUENCE
LAUREN HUTTON

DESPITE LIVING in Europe and being married to an Englishman, I consider myself typically American. In that regard, no one inspires me more than Lauren Hutton, whose looks and style have barely changed over the past four decades, and who epitomizes the very essence of classic American chic. I am inspired by her love of sportswear, her ability to make the most casual clothes look elegant and her steady relevance in nearly every decade in which I can find a photo of her. But beyond the iconic status of her style is the remarkably strong presence of the person who inhabits it—the gap in her teeth, the straw backpack she never leaves at home, the naturally curly hair, the bazillion trillion watts of her smile. For me, Lauren Hutton is the whole package.

Opposite: Lauren Hutton strikes the perfect balance of classic and bohemian.

117

TRY ANYTHING THAT GRABS YOUR ATTENTION— YOU GOTTA START SOMEWHERE!

FROM A STYLE point of view, I spent all of my twenties being a chameleon. I took influence and inspiration from wherever it came, and tried it on. At twenty-two, I was what some people now call a "gallerina," one of the well-raised, polite girls pretty enough to charm billionaires into buying art at blue-chip galleries.

Before I'd even arrived at Gagosian, I had the gallerina uniform down pat. Patricia Herrera, my college roommate for two years, was born into a family of fashion royalty (she is Carolina's daughter), lived in New York City, and at age twenty already had her own personal style thoroughly worked out. I was so impressed at the time by the flashiest of my fellow students—the girls who wore Marc Jacobs for Perry Ellis grunge, head-to-toe Chanel and hot-off-the-runway Ralph Lauren. But I realize now that the person who influenced me the most in the long run was Patricia. She had beautiful clothes, but they were not overtly attention-seeking or even recognizable as belonging to any certain designer. She was casual, unpretentious, and yet chic in an elegant and understated way.

Patricia taught me about buying pants at Joseph, the tiny English boutique on Madison Avenue that had fifty styles of perfectly cut,

Opposite: That time when my Tuleh pants split right down the middle at an art opening, 2000. Photo by Christopher.

119

stretch trousers in cotton, wool tweed, leather, and even pleather, for those, like me, on a more modest college budget. Patricia would wear her chic Joseph pants with Converse All-Stars way before it was cool to wear tailoring with sneakers. I could afford only one pair of Josephs at a time, but I made it a goal to save up so I could buy one pair each season. Soon I had a nice little collection of perfect pants.

Patricia also taught me about Free Lance boots. Free Lance was a shoe company that had a boutique in SoHo, and they'd nailed the perfect jodhpur boot with a chunky two-inch heel. They were casual enough to wear every day but nice enough to wear to work or a job interview. They were at the top of my price range so I had only one pair, in black leather. They were classic.

And finally, Patricia introduced me to Equipment shirts. I was familiar with the brand because my mom wore their shirts, and until then I assumed that I couldn't afford anything my mom wore. And I was right, but when I got my job at Gagosian, I went to Equipment the day before I was due to start and bought myself a black washed silk military-style shirt that I still wear today.

So in I walked on my first day at the gallery in my new Equipment shirt, black pleather Joseph pants, and only boots. It was an intimidating crowd in an even more intimidating environment, but my outfit gave me confidence, as if to say "I belong here."

After I left Gagosian and went to work at Frédéric Fekkai, it was the first time I had any disposable income. My healthier wallet gave me the chance to experiment more with trendy and frivolous pieces. I bought two pairs of stiletto boots at the Stephane Kélian sample sale, a Jamin Puech fabric bag with ostrich feather trim on a business trip to Paris, and a few embroidered slip dresses from Ghost (all iconic nineties pieces). I'd also discovered the unique and affordable finds to be had at the Paris flea market: silk flower pins, sequin headbands, and engraved gold hoop earrings. Worn with my more tailored Joseph and Zara pieces, it was a good mix of classic masculinity and more whimsical feminine pieces.

While I was at Fekkai, I got a call from *Vogue* asking to photograph me for their "Best-Dressed List." Needless to say, I was over

the moon. I was a humble shopper, meaning that my clothing budget was just a fraction of what many of my friends and contemporaries in fashion spent (and without all the freebies a magazine editor receives), but the necessity to find things in unconventional places had made my style unique, and I was proud to be recognized for that.

André Leon Talley was the stylist on the shoot, and he thought it would be fun to put me in a huge, and I really mean *huge*, Tuleh ballgown. It was a black strapless cotton dress with a fitted bodice and a giant, crinoline-supported voluminous skirt covered in bows. Gisele Bündchen had worn the same dress in white in another magazine, and I couldn't believe that I would have the chance to wear something so over the top, so high fashion. When I put it on, I was transformed, and André took one look at me and said, "You're keeping that." After a polite protest on my part, André called the designers and announced that I should keep the dress. Being young designers on the rise, and obviously beholden to *Vogue*, what could they say other than "yes"?

The reality of owning that dress was way less glamorous than the fantasy of it. Or maybe it was glamorous in a Holly Golightly kind of way. The dress really was *huge*, and it weighed a ton. It didn't fit in the tiny closet in my walk-up apartment, and so for three weeks it lay across my sofa, covering the entire thing so you couldn't actually sit down. It also dawned on me that I wouldn't have many opportunities to wear this behemoth of a fairy-tale dress. A few weeks later, Josh Patner, one of the Tuleh designers, called and sheepishly explained that the dress, which had a whopping $10,000 retail value, had been ordered by a client, and that to make another one would be prohibitively expensive for them. He asked if I'd allow them to sell my dress to the client, and in exchange, they would let me come to the showroom and order anything I wanted from the collection. We instantly bonded in our mutual relief as I responded with a resounding "Yes!" and made plans to go to the studio.

I'd seen a friend wearing Tuleh a few months prior, and then seen more of the collection on the racks at Bergdorf Goodman. It

was one of the most original brands I'd discovered in a long time. In the midst of all the grungy gloom and restrained minimalism of the nineties, Tuleh was exuberant and happy and colorful and feminine. At the showroom I ordered ruffled floral blouses, sexy secretary windowpane-checked skirts, a cropped fox-fur vest, menswear-tailored classic wool pants, and a stunning red chiffon cocktail dress. I felt like I'd found my look, and I couldn't get over my luck in receiving all these clothes for free.

Just as my Tuleh love affair was beginning, I left my job at Fekkai and went to work at Hogan, an Italian accessories brand owned by Tod's that played the role of its younger, sportier little sister. (More on working at Hogan in the next chapter.)

My style while working at Hogan was inspired by the tomboy, preppy look of the brand, but in my off-duty time, I loved the contrast of being the ultragirly, feminine Tuleh girl. Designers Josh Patner and Bryan Bradley lived around the corner from me in the West Village, and while I was committed to working at Hogan during the week, I'd wander over to their apartment on Sundays to talk about inspiration, fabrics for their next collection, and what was missing from my wardrobe. I longed to be that glamorous girl that the Tuleh clothes encouraged me to be. I wanted to wear heels, curl my hair, and wear red lipstick. I wanted the pleasure of dolling myself up every morning.

And then, life took me by surprise. I got pregnant! I'd been with Christopher for four years and I knew I wanted to spend my life with him, and so we decided to get married. Trouble was, my job at Hogan required me to travel to Europe for at least a week every month, and often longer. Suddenly my priorities changed drastically, and I knew that my current lifestyle wasn't going to work for me.

Hogan, being the Italian family-oriented company that they are, offered me a generous consulting gig, allowing me to do much of the same work—forecasting trends, giving design direction, and suggesting new product ideas—as a part-time job with no travel requirements. When the deal was sealed, I realized I'd have the best

of all worlds: I could keep my steady and secure day job, be home to nurture my new family, and work with Tuleh (who could afford only to pay me in clothes!) in my spare time.

It all worked perfectly for a while, until I found myself struggling to find a balance. I knew the time had come to make a decision. While the Hogan job definitely represented a part of me, I knew that the work I did at Tuleh was a much bigger opportunity for my personal creative expression, and I convinced my husband to temporarily support me while I devoted myself completely to making it enough of a success to be able to afford to hire me.

Chatting on the phone at home in my favorite Tuleh blouse, 2002.

Above: One of my favorite Tuleh shows, 2000. Opposite: Wearing a dress from that same show to Emilia Fanjul's wedding rehearsal in the Dominican Republic, 2002.

With my plan in mind, I asked Josh and Bryan out to dinner. We went to the restaurant at Industria, the trendy photography studio complex in our mutual West Village neighborhood. I always had such a laugh with the two of them. Josh was extroverted, emotional and outspoken—he dreamed big and was passionate about everything he loved. He had an idea a minute and was never hesitant to express them. He was also wickedly funny and did the best impressions of people. At Tuleh, he came up with the inspiration, the big idea behind the collection, and then faithfully saw it through to completion, managing every detail. He was also a brilliant stylist. Any look I could make or Bryan could make, Josh could make better. Bryan, on the other hand, was far more reserved and shy. He chose his words carefully and expressed them sincerely. He loved reading and was careful about the friends he chose. And he was a brilliant designer. He could design anything. He could dream up a dress, sketch it, create the pattern, and fit it with a sense of natural ease that impressed everyone in the studio and subsequently in the fashion world. At the end of the dinner that night, I asked them if they would take me on in the studio full-time, and they graciously and enthusiastically accepted.

My title at Tuleh was creative director, but more specifically, my job was to be the female voice—the embodiment of the ideal customer—in every aspect of the conception, design, execution, presentation, and sales of each collection. I shared with Josh and Bryan what was missing from my closet, what I was in the mood

That's me on the right (chatting with Sally Albemarle and Francisco Costa), wearing a Tuleh gown at a Guggenheim benefit honoring Azzedine Alaïa, 2004.

for, what I wanted to wear. I helped them choose fabrics and come up with new silhouettes and proportions. I tried on muslins and test-drove newly finished pieces. I stayed at the studio until three A.M. every night in the week before their shows styling looks, accessorizing them, proposing ideas for hair and makeup, choosing the right model for the right outfit. When all that was said and done, I always wore (showed off!) my favorite outfit from the collection for the sales meetings with the stores and eventually, when we discovered that I was good at selling clothes to the clients, traveled around the country working the trunk shows at Saks and Neiman.

Every single day I was at Tuleh was an invitation to act out some fantasy about myself. Josh and Bryan loved seeing me arrive in the studio wearing the clothes that they had designed but that I had styled to create my own look. One dress was made of red silk printed with black and white stars. I showed up at Aerin Lauder's son's birthday party wearing it with black point d'esprit stockings and black leather Manolo Blahnik pumps with a white grosgrain ribbon on the toe, and red lipstick to match the dress. To Anh Duong's art opening, I wore a pair of purple floral-print cotton men's tailored trousers with a feminine puff-sleeve blouse that had sequined lilacs all over it. As if that weren't enough of an outfit, I put on my vintage purple silk YSL pumps with a giant bow on the toe. Karma must have wanted to bring me down a notch, though, because my pants split right down the middle of my butt halfway through the evening.

Tuleh was both an ideal job and style inspiration for three thrilling years, but I grew tired of expending so much of my creative energy with no salary in return. The company had grown a lot while I was there, but there was always a reason why they couldn't afford to pay me even half the salary I'd been earning at Hogan. So, after a period of heartbreak and coming to terms with my disappointment, we eventually parted ways.

At this point I was turning thirty, and as I reflected back on my twenties, I was anxious to make sense of where I had started and where I was then, both in terms of my style and my career. I was dedicated to fashion and I was making headway. I had learned an awful lot, but had had a string of one- and two-year jobs that all seemed to lead to something else or arrive at a dead end. I was tired of being someone new all the time, and with the birth of my second child, I didn't have the energy to invent new looks or dedicate my workday to a project I wasn't passionate about. What I felt confident in, however, was how much I had come to know about myself through the clothes I had worn, and how valuable the cumulative experiences and relationships I had created for myself in fashion, photography, and the art world were to my future career plans, whatever they might be.

SOFIA COPPOLA

IF I COULD pick one person to swap wardrobes with, it would be Sofia. Her style is a balanced combination of evolved good taste, refined simplicity, classic chic, with just a tiny bit of trend thrown in. I can't imagine she ever looks back at outfits she has worn in the past and asks herself, *What was I thinking?* Often when I need a quick break from my work, I Google Sofia so I can save and file her latest outfits. (Yes, I am a bit of a cyberstalker when it comes to her.) Or sometimes I look through my saved Sofia files—black dresses, NYC apartment, flowers, hotel in Italy, Louis Vuitton bag, nineties style, L.A. house—just to give myself a high sartorial bar to aspire to. She may just be my favorite of all style setters.

Opposite: No one makes simple, classic clothes look so chic!

129

AMY ASTLEY

AMY IS the editor in chief of *Teen Vogue* and has held that position as long as we have been friends, which is now more than a decade. Before I knew Amy well, I always admired her glamorous and well-defined personal style, but I didn't get to really know her until we became summer neighbors. When I first visited Amy at her beach house in Long Island, I was so impressed and relieved that the house wasn't all "editor-in-chief-ified." Don't get me wrong—her house was *awesome*, charming and super-stylish, but it was relatable, too. Her outside furniture was a bit rusty (as is mine), she had her toddler's crib in the living room, and she herself was casually dressed in a batik Gap sundress. Amy's casual and laid-back lifestyle outside of fashion gave me confidence in embracing the reality of my own.

When we go to a picnic at the beach, which we often do, we make our sandwiches, schlep our beach chairs, and read the Sunday paper while our kids play in the sand and chase one another into the ocean. I've got on my $50 Rainbow flip-flops and my J.Crew shorts, and Amy is wearing her daughter's tie-dye shirt from American Eagle with the same Gap sundress, now worn as a skirt. Once Amy brought a Prada beach bag that she'd gotten at a sample sale—it had the most gorgeous orange crocodile trim on it—and we came back from a walk to see that the tide had soaked all our belongings. "That is the last time I try to be chic at the beach!" she declared. That's what I love about Amy's style—it inspires me to know when it's time to be chic and when it's time to be real.

I have asked Amy about her fashion philosophy and I always keep in mind what she said. She explained to me that, as a person, she feels open and approachable and she wants her clothes to reflect that whether she's at the beach or in the front row of a fashion show.

"The last thing I want my style to say is 'Fashion person: Stand back!'" says Amy.

Left: Amy and her daughter Ingrid visiting me in the Adirondacks. I love Amy's Stephen Sprouse for Louis Vuitton scarf worn with a nineties L.L. Bean anorak! Opposite: Amy in chic fashion-editor mode.

MISTAKES ARE OKAY, AS LONG AS YOU LEARN FROM THEM

MY FIRST BIG career failure happened while I was creative director of Hogan. Creative director is a big title for a twenty-five-year-old. I'm still not sure how I got it. It may simply have been because I had the nerve to ask for it. What happened was, I was at Fekkai, and when the first collection of bags I had worked on came out, they received a good deal of press from fashion magazines, and Emanuele Della Valle took notice. Emanuele is the son of Diego Della Valle, owner of Tod's and Hogan, and he was managing the U.S. side of the Hogan business. After following what I did for another season, he called me in for an interview. We chatted and he consequently proposed that I work with the design team on expanding the collection to better suit the American market, and also, with my photography background, work on putting together the team (photographer, stylist, set designer, art director, hair, makeup) for the ad campaigns. At twenty-four, Emanuele had just about as much experience as I had (meaning an impressive amount for our age, but still not much), and together we confidently moved in the direction of our ambition.

On average I spent a week each month in Italy at the leather factory, working with the design team on new products and future col-

Opposite: My son, Zach, and I modeling for Tod's in a photo by one of my heroes, Elliott Erwitt. I organized the shoot as one of my consulting projects for the Della Valles and was thrilled to be featured in it as well.

133

lections, sometimes seeing evidence of my ideas in the collection, and other times not. Sometimes I would leave Italy thinking I had finally made some headway, and then I would return again weeks later to see that many of the changes I had requested had been ignored and progress I had made had been changed according to the design team's liking. Other times, I would return to the factory to see an idea I had that had come to life just as I had imagined it. I would wonder aloud how the bag might look with a different color stitching or with shorter handles, and the bag would be whisked off to the factory and returned just moments later with the changes I had requested completed. That aspect of the design process was immensely satisfying.

On the advertising front, however, I had vastly more weight and influence. Diego had entrusted Emanuele and me to conceptualize, produce, and execute the Hogan ad campaign from New York, something he rarely allowed. Diego was so personally and professionally invested in the ads (I would be, too, if all that money was coming from me!) that he usually never let the ad campaign be shot too far away from his command central in Milan. But Emanuele was his son, and so I think he was trying to give him some independence.

Everything had come together so well. We hired a fashion dream team, including photographer Nathaniel Goldberg and stylist Emmanuelle Alt (now the editor in chief of French *Vogue*) and models Karolina Kurkova and Raquel Zimmermann (then at the very start of their careers), and we chose an inspired location— the world-famous but out-of-commission Eero Saarinen–designed terminal at JFK. Because the Hogan collection was based around sneakers and an active lifestyle, we thought the idea of travel fit perfectly into the concept of the brand.

The day before the shoot, Emanuele and I were feeling excited and confident. We had a great idea in place, and after careful planning and research had hired an excellent team to execute it. Clothes were packed, models were hired, access permissions were granted. All that was left to do that afternoon was to walk through the actual terminal with the photographer and the production company to figure out where each shot would take place. Susan, the produc-

tion head, had arrived before us and came to greet us with a grim expression on her face. "The place isn't in great condition." It was in that precise moment that the entire shoot fell apart. Enthusiastic as we all were that it would be fine, the truth was that the whole terminal was made from white tiles that were dirty and cracked. If you shot from a distance, it would have been okay, but we were shooting shoes—*up close!*—and the place just wasn't up to par for a close-up. I tried so hard to convince everyone that surely we could just retouch the flaws, but in the end the producer and the photographer put their collective foot down. It wasn't gonna work.

At this point, everyone was on a plane or in some sort of transit, day rates were guaranteed, and the shoot was confirmed. We were having the shoot whether we wanted to or not. So we settled for a much newer but far less stylish terminal at JFK. I was both crushed and scared, and Emanuele was rightfully pissed off the whole day of the shoot. We both knew right away that it wasn't what we'd envisioned. It wasn't a strong or graphic enough background for the concept we had imagined, and no amount of styling or clever camera angles was going to fix it. The mood on the set was gloomy—everyone was acutely aware of things not going as we all had hoped and apprehensive about the part each of us had played in that. I was sure I would be fired immediately once word got back to Milan. I kept reassuring myself with thoughts of all the people I had known who had been dismissed from their jobs and went on to be successful in other capacities.

In the end, the ad campaign was thrown in the trash, wasting hundreds of thousands of dollars. But by some miracle, I was spared. The production manager was blamed for not discovering the sad state of the terminal sooner, the art director was dismissed for not thinking up a miraculous solution, and the ad campaign duties were handed back to Italy. I felt so much better when I learned that this wasn't the first or last time Diego had chucked out an ad campaign regardless of the talent he had entrusted it to. But still—the pictures weren't good and it had happened on my watch. While I finished out the year of my contract contributing

135

ideas for design and advertising, I never felt very effective in my job at Hogan. I did feel like I had a lot to offer, but it was clear to everyone involved that the way my job was set up wasn't working.

After a year, we agreed that I would be a consultant to the company, and this arrangement worked infinitely better. In fact, working with the Della Valles in subsequent years—at Hogan, Tod's, and Roger Vivier—would be one of the most satisfying experiences I had in my time as a consultant. Among the highlights was getting to work with my old friend Bruno Frisoni, who had since become creative director of Roger Vivier, and doing a projet and then a whole ad campaign for Tod's with one of my photography heroes, Elliot Erwitt.

Diego is an incredibly focused and creative businessman, and his story as the son of an Italian cobbler who became the eventual owner of an entire empire is one of fashion's greatest success stories. I have also been inspired by Emanuele's cultural curiosity and appreciation of Americana. As an Italian he sees American life and style with completely fresh eyes and gives me a new way of seeing things I may have dismissed as being too familiar. In his own career path, he has gone on to revolutionize how we interact with fashion in digital media. I continued consulting for Emanuele and Diego on and off for many years, successfully and happily, and I consider it a real achievement that we were able to eventually find a formula for working together that made sense for all of us.

Emanuele and I can now laugh about our disastrous time together at Hogan. It's so easy to see now that we were handed too much responsibility too quickly. But God, it felt so terrible at the time. I felt powerless and pathetic. And I was scared all the time—scared of failure, scared of being fired, scared of being blamed.

The experience of my Hogan disaster made me understand the importance of communication, working relationships, and company structure in a way that I hadn't before. In future working arrangements I would spend hours with my lawyer before agreeing to anything, making sure that my potential employer and I both understood each other's expectations, requirements, and working style. This habit of up-front understanding has never failed me since.

My T. Anthony luggage, Céline bag, and Chanel jacket at the airport in Milan.

FASHION LESSON NO. 4
PACKING FASHION

THE FIRST time I went to Milan for fashion week was when I was working at Hogan, age twenty-five. I had to pack ten days' and evenings' worth of great outfits. As I worked for a designer, I wouldn't be going to other designers' shows, but I would attend all the presentations and events hosted by Hogan and their parent company, Tod's, and I would have endless breakfasts, lunches, and dinners with fashion editors from both American and foreign magazines and newspapers. Because Hogan is an accessories company, the outfits I chose were based around the various shoes I wanted to make sure editors saw me wearing. It being Hogan, I had a variety of "fashion sneakers" packed, as well as a pair of fur-covered boots, a wedge-heel "secretary" loafer, and purple snakeskin pumps from Tod's. I also packed a half dozen handbags—some sporty totes

from Hogan and some more refined shoulder bags and clutches from Tod's. Then, of course, there were all the trousers, sweaters, dresses, skirts, and coats that went with the all-important accessories. I didn't plan—I just selected from my closet everything I thought I might need that week and threw it in two oversize wheelie bags.

I knew I was in trouble as soon as I was leaving my apartment. If you can't even get from your front door to a taxi unassisted, then you know your traveling experience is going to be a nightmare. Collecting my bags and going through customs in Milan was the worst. The bags were too big to fit on one trolley and so I dragged them both behind me on their wheels, one in each hand, and did my best to steer them both in the same direction at once. It took hours to unpack at the hotel, and most of my beautiful handbags had been crushed by the journey. Of course I didn't even end up wearing half of what I'd packed during the trip. I can look back now and see that I was nervous, wanting so much to look and feel good, and wanting to be prepared. I can also see that packing like that is not the way to feel prepared, secure, or more relaxed.

After that trip, I made some rules that I have lived by ever since. These rules have gotten me through vacations, weekend stays, work trips, and, most no-tably, seventeen days of business travel through Milan and Paris, going to non-stop fashion shows, cocktail parties, and meetings feeling well dressed, organized, and at ease in the airport (well, as much as you can be). Here they are:

1. Lay out a few things you are most excited to take with you. Your favorite new dress, your chicest coat, your go-everywhere blouse, the shoes you bought last week . . .

2. Come up with a color story around these pieces. Does everything go with black shoes? Are you packing mostly neutrals? Or is it a colorblocking moment?

If I am going on a short trip, I will limit myself to two pairs of shoes in the same color—flats and heels. Then I choose a bag that coordinates with the shoes, and maybe a clutch for the evening.

On longer trips, I will pack two or three accessory "color stories" (and usually neutral, like brown or black), but no more than that. Limiting accessories by sticking to this principle makes a huge difference in packing. Accessories are heavy, take up space, and often get scuffed or misshapen in your bag.

3. Layer in the more useful items—camisoles, tights, sweaters, cardigans—based on what you will need to wear with the favorite pieces you have chosen in step 1. I usually lay all this out on my bed so I can see how everything is coming together.

4. Then put everything in the suitcase you intend to travel with. Pack your toiletries, your computer chargers, your socks and undies, your exercise gear, and then when all of that is in, if you have more space, pack one or two things that weren't priorities but still work within your color story. I might pack an extra coat I didn't think I had room for, or a few more skirts.

5. Never take more than one main suitcase with you when you travel, unless you are going away for more than three weeks. And if you are away for only a week, just take a carry-on (easier in summer than in winter). Your mental health will thank you for it.

Some people make all their outfits in advance and take Polaroids of them when traveling. This takes the fun and spontaneity out of getting dressed for me. Even when traveling I still like to feel that nervous energy of not knowing what I am going to wear in the morning. I find that if I think some outfits through in my head, plan my general color stories, and include the crucial things I need and/or want to take, mixed in with some practical and versatile basics, then I am set to travel stress free and in style.

THE BRILLIANCE OF WHITE SHOES

WHEN I GOT married, I asked Christian Louboutin to make me a timeless and simple yet sexy pair of white pumps. He knew what I meant—pointed toe, skinny 95-cm heel, just enough toe cleavage. I asked for them to be made in peau de soie, the classic silk used for an evening shoe, but he thought that might make them too tasteful. Is a white shoe ever tasteful? I didn't think so, but I told Christian to go with his instinct, which was to make them in white moiré taffeta.

The shoes were absolutely perfect on the day—a dash of class (my wedding dress) with an oh-so-subtle dash of trash (the shoes)—and they miraculously managed to remain pristine white. But what do you do with a pair of white moiré stilettos? My first instinct was to dye them—they'd make a stunning black evening pump. But I already had similar shoes in black. And brown. And electric blue. And fire-engine red. Because Christian did the shoes for the Tuleh shows and I got to keep the leftovers, I already had an enviable rainbow of fabulous pumps in my closet. So I reluctantly decided to leave the white ones white.

It wasn't until I owned a pair of white pumps that I realized how useful they could be. Tired of wearing a black dress with black heels? Wear white heels. Don't have the right color sandal to wear with your summer florals? Wear white sandals. Looking to add a little irreverence to an otherwise straightforward look? Again, white is the answer.

I wore my white silk pumps so much that I wore them out. Next, I tried white suede pumps. They were killer, but they lasted only three wears before looking more gray than white. At the moment, I'm loving my white leather ballet flats, and I just bought a pair of pristine white Converse for summer, having opted for a more tasteful off-white version in the past. But why do we have to be tasteful all the time? It's far more fun—and chic!—to be daring.

Opposite: I love how the white flowers on Taylor Tomasi Hill's Thom Browne jacket balance out the Céline white heels, which make the look.

FAKE IT 'TIL YOU
MAKE IT

THE FIRST TIME I appeared in *Vogue* was while I was working at Gagosian. My oldest friend, Celerie, rang me up and said, "Amanda, your feet are in *Vogue*!" The magazine had done a trend page on brightly colored pants and I'd worn a pair of hot orange Joseph ones to a fashion party with Christopher. They were mostly cotton with a shiny satin tuxedo stripe down the side of each leg. Sounds hideous now, right? Well, *Vogue* had snapped my pants, but because I was unknown to the fashion world at that time, they cut off my head and just featured the lower half of my body, including my toes peeking out from my open-toe stilettos. I do, in fact, have recognizable feet, and not in a good way. Many people's second toes are longer than their first, as mine are, but in fact my third toes, while smaller than my second toes, are also longer than my first, making a kind of handlike silhouette. I was delighted, however, to be featured in *Vogue*—in any form. I also really appreciated Celerie in that moment—I am lucky to have a friend who knows me so well she can recognize me by my fugly toes!

The next time I was in *Vogue*, they zeroed in on my feather-trimmed handbag. My head made it in this time, but my name

Opposite: Me (in Oscar de la Renta) and Zach, as Batman, in our Lower East Side apartment, shot for the debut issue of Vogue Living, 2006.

didn't. I was "girl at a party," or something like that. This sudden attention to my clothes made me all the more excited to get dressed for parties. As usual, I pushed myself to buy designers I could barely afford. For one particular party, a *Vogue* celebration at Balthazar of Oprah's cover debut, I went to Calypso, a trendy new boutique in Nolita that sold things at just under designer price range. I bought two Tracy Feith Indian-inspired paisley slip dresses to layer together. I then went around the corner and bought a pair of brown leather chunky-heeled sandals from Sigerson Morrison, the new shoe store everyone was talking about. When putting it all together on the night of, I slipped a silk flower that I'd bought at the flea market in my ponytail. It was the perfect final touch. I arrived at Balthazar that night with Christopher, and we were snapped by the photographers as soon as we walked in. I felt so good the whole night. I had a wonderful boyfriend, was at a glamorous party, and loved what I was wearing. When the next issue of *Vogue* came out, there I was—my full body was photographed this time, and my name was printed with my picture. It was my first official photograph in the magazine, and I was proud as could be.

My next appearance in *Vogue* would be in a more official capacity. It was after I'd left Gagosian and was temporarily helping out in my mother's interior design office. I was sitting at the drafting board, on the phone with a fabric mill, when my mother tiptoed in and mouthed, "Someone from *Vogue* is on the phone!" I quickly hung up and picked up the other line. It was Plum Sykes.

"Darling, would you like to be in *Vogue*?" she asked in her posh English accent.

"Um . . . yes!" I replied, not even sure what she was asking me.

"Okay, great. Go to Pier 59 Studios tomorrow at one P.M."

I showed up with no idea what to expect. I was especially nervous because I was still growing out a short haircut and it was in a particularly awkward phase. After announcing myself at reception, I was led into a photo studio that felt like home—I had shot there many, many times when working with Patrick. On the dry-erase board next to the entrance, the names Steven Meisel and

Grace Coddington caught my eye, and my heart pounded in my chest. *I must be in the wrong place*, I thought.

But sure enough, my friend Anne Christensen (a freelance stylist who'd been Grace's assistant for many years) wandered over and brought me up to speed on the shoot. Grace was styling and Steven was shooting the "12 Days of Christmas." And I was going to be one of the "social girls" representing the "nine ladies dancing." We'd all be wearing Chanel couture. HOLY. SHIT. Holy shit! Holy shit! Holy shit!

Garren, the legendary high-fashion hair guru, did the best he could with my hair. He gave it a bit of a trim at the bottom and blew it out stick straight (it was the nineties, after all). The

My Steven Meisel/Grace Coddington/Chanel Haute Couture moment in Vogue, *1997. I don't think it ever got much better than this!*

145

equally famous makeup artist Diane Kendal gave me a smoky eye and more makeup than I'd ever worn in my entire life, and Grace chose a beaded and embroidered camisole top with matching skirt for me to wear. I felt cooler than I'd ever felt but still so much less cool than all the other "ladies dancing," who included Julian Schnabel's daughters, the Ronson girls, Fernanda Niven, and supermodel Shalom Harlow. The worst was when Steven asked us to dance. Sober dancing in a cold studio in front of intimidating girls was not the way to bring out the best in me. Eventually, we loosened up (a bit) and the picture came together. When it was published, the expression on my face wasn't the most flattering, but I looked like I was having a good time.

The next *Vogue* call came when I was happily settled into my job at Fekkai. They were doing a best-dressed list organized by industries, and, as previously mentioned on page 120, I was asked to be included, representing the beauty industry. The shoot conflicted with a big work meeting, but it was decided by Frédéric that it would be great exposure for the company. I showed up for the shoot at the Mercer Hotel. Pamela Hanson was shooting it, and she had a vision of me jumping on the bed in one of the giant ball-gowns that stylist André Leon Talley had selected for me. I jumped on the bed tentatively at first, and then I really started to enjoy it. The more relaxed I became, the more excited they got, and after a few minutes it was like a switch went off inside of me. I let go completely and allowed myself to enjoy the moment. It was my first taste of being empowered in front of the camera, and I loved it.

The photo was . . . *expressive*, to say the least. Plum called me before I'd even seen it. "I'm not sure you're going to like your photo, darling. You look a bit mad in it." My heart sank, and I was prepared for the worst. But when I finally saw it, I liked the photo. I was in midair, the giant dress flying up around me, my head tilted back and my mouth open with laughter. It's not super-flattering, but I look happy and it reminds me of the fun I had that day.

The next shoot wasn't nearly so successful. Again I was grouped in with a selection of socially and professionally notable young

women, Laura Bailey, China Chow, Lauren Bush, and Kidada Jones among them. Camilla Nickerson was the stylist, Elaine Constantine was the photographer, and we shot on location in East Hampton. Elaine's style was to capture movement with a big flash so we were constantly lunging at the camera, or asked to laugh on command, or asked to splash around in the pool. This all seemed fine until we were asked to wear *tiny* bikinis. I caught a glimpse of one of the Polaroids and it so horrified me that I discreetly approached Camilla and said, "I really don't feel comfortable wearing such a tiny bikini for these pictures. The Polaroids are *not* flattering." She wouldn't hear it and reassured me that it would all be retouched and the pictures would be great. It was too late for me, though. I'd already entered a shame spiral. Thank God the pictures never ran. A friend at *Vogue* told me that Anna deemed them "too young," and apparently they served as a mock spread for a test issue of the forthcoming *Teen Vogue*.

Being in *Vogue* is valuable to any fashion brand. If you are in the magazine at all regularly, designers want to dress you. I traded on this for many years, and the abundance of borrowed clothes allowed me to experiment more freely with my style and create close relationships with designers. But as I earned more money, I made the decision to buy more and borrow less. It was a more honest relationship with myself and a better way to develop and nurture a true sense of style. Borrowing had been a fun way to experiment in my twenties, but once I entered my thirties, I wanted to be more focused and disciplined. I also wanted more simplicity in getting dressed.

My plan worked, and my style became more focused. Then *Vogue* called again wanting to feature me in a shopping story in the editorial section of the September Issue, a big honor that required all sorts of assurances from me that I wouldn't be photographed for any other magazine that month. I boarded a plane to Palm Beach with Mark Holgate (the writer), Alexandra Kotur (the sittings editor), and Jonathan Becker (the photographer). *Vogue* wanted me to lead them around to my favorite vintage shopping haunts in Palm Beach (of which there are many) and then photograph me in some

of my favorite purchases. Back in New York, I'd then show them some of the big splurges in my own closet and also some of my favorite cheap chic resources. This was probably the most meaningful photo shoot I'd ever done because *Vogue* was validating the way I'd shopped all my life: a few special designer purchases, mixed in with the best of H&M and Zara, mixed in with vintage pieces bought in Palm Beach or handed down from my eccentric great-aunt Molly (read more about her on page 186). In the past, I felt that I was playing a role when I was being photographed, but in this story, I felt like me. The portraits taken for this shoot are my favorite ever taken of me, and I treasure them.

Not even a year later, *Vogue* called once more, yet again for the September Issue. They were doing a story about New York ladies striking out with their own original projects (they called it "The Selling of the Socialite") and they wanted to include a section about me writing *I Love Your Style*. I'd be photographed at Christopher's family farm in England. Once given the tour, Jonathan and Alexandra decided they wanted to photograph me by a lake that actually belonged to our next-door neighbor. I did my own hair and makeup and wore a Grecian-inspired Zac Posen gown. It's a beautiful portrait, but I look a bit tired in it. Note to self: Believe people when they tell you that you need to wear more makeup than you think for a photograph.

After that double September Issue whammy, I didn't expect to be featured in *Vogue* again for a very long time, if at all. But surprisingly, Hamish Bowles called up one day, confiding that he was working on the debut issue of *Vogue Living*, and he asked if he could come see my apartment. The insanity began right then and there. If you've ever had someone you revere come to look at your house, you'll know what I mean. Decorating homes is something I've never considered myself particularly good at. I'd decorated our New York apartment in my Tuleh years after a phase when I was obsessed with the English decorator David Hicks. This all translated to lots of very bold print and color: pink rugs, turquoise paintings, brown velvet, silver lamé, pop-inspired paintings by my

husband. It was certainly a statement, but one I quickly grew bored with. In fact, I grew tired of the whole look before I'd had the chance (and the funds) to even finish decorating.

After hours and hours of manic midnight styling, cleaning, and reorganizing, Hamish came to take a look. I held my breath as Hamish walked around, and I tried to be as positive as I possibly could. I told him how I bought the group of five paintings in the living room from a vintage shop on the Lower East Side, how all the collages in the hallway were Valentines that Christopher and I had made for each other, how I had cashed in my entire wedding registry credit to afford Pratesi sheets for all the beds, how the kitschy wallpaper in the bathroom was an ode to my childhood in Palm Beach, etc.

My desperate enthusiasm must have worked, because Hamish called the next morning to say he wanted to shoot it. There was also the small matter of styling me for the shoot. When Hamish came over for the fitting, he looked at me sheepishly as he unzipped the garment bags and announced, "I have a vision." He then pulled out *giant* gowns from Oscar de la Renta and Isaac Mizrahi that perfectly matched the colors of my apartment. You would have thought, given the style of my apartment, that I'd have loved them, but they were *so not me*. I gamely put them on while the hairstylist teased my hair up into an impromptu sixties froth, and before I could protest, Miles Aldridge, the photographer, entered the room and pronounced my look "Brilliant!" I was tongue-tied, and confused, and very, very far away from looking like myself.

I went into the bathroom, looked at my drag queen–like self in the mirror, and realized before even wondering how to get myself out of this look that there was no going back. I said to myself, "This is *Vogue*. You are in the hands of a stylist you respect and a photographer you admire. *Let go*. If the pictures are ridiculous, they just won't be published." I accepted that Anna would be the final judge. If she liked the high kitsch, sixties fantasy take on me, then so be it; I could live with that. And if she didn't, then I knew I'd be saved because no one would ever see the photos.

After the shoot I called Miranda, who is a contributing editor at *Vogue* and also my husband's ex-wife. Over the years we had slowly become good friends. I confided in her that I really wasn't sure about the photos, but that if *Vogue* was happy, then I'd be happy. She called back a week or so later and said that Anna had loved them. I tried not to worry about it after that.

When the pictures came out in *Vogue Living*, they were wonderfully over the top. It was obvious that the shoot was a fashion fantasy, starring me in my house, and it was exceedingly obvious that I didn't *actually* dress that way. Looking through the story with my mom, we shared a laugh. As an interior decorator, she was proud to see me and my house in the company of Jennifer Lopez, Aerin Lauder, and Samantha Boardman.

What I learned from all this is that being in *Vogue* is a powerful thing, and I am grateful for both the experience and the benefits it bestowed upon me. The interests and ambitions I had, the limitations I faced, and the quirky way I found my way into the fashion world all forced me to do things my own way, on my own terms, and *Vogue*'s celebration of that gave me a belief in the satisfaction and ultimate recognition of doing things unconventionally that will stay with me for a lifetime.

LEARN HOW TO SMILE FOR A PHOTO
(IT TOOK ME FIFTEEN YEARS!)

FOR MANY years, when people met me, they would often tell me that I was prettier in real life than in photographs. They were right! It took me a long time to learn how to show my best self in pictures. I used to tease my friend Anh, who, as we were entering a party, would always say out loud, "remember the half smile." This directive reminded her not to smile too big in a photo, as she felt it made her look goofy. As much as we talked and laughed about it, I never took this advice to heart. Not only would I smile big with my mouth, but I would also smile big with my eyes. The result? I looked like a deer in the headlights in nearly every photograph that was taken of me in my twenties. I always look way overexcited. Not cute. Not sexy. Just slightly out of my mind. I don't remember what the final straw was, but it must have been after a particularly bad picture of me ran in some publication that I decided I would practice my camera smile in the mirror until I got it right. I started with a half smile. But the result was smug and insincere. What I realized was that the problem wasn't my smile—like I alluded to earlier, it was my eyes! Every time I smiled, my eyes would widen. I think I learned to do this full-face smile as a young child, because every photo I have from about age four on has this kind of ecstatic, manic expression. So I worked on a full smile with my mouth, but only a half smile with my eyes. It took me a while to get it right, but now it comes naturally, and I have looked better in photographs ever since.

Opposite: My Francesco Scavullo moment for Harper's Bazaar. I'm such a fan of his seventies and eighties beauty portraits and couldn't be happier to have one of my own. This photo was included in a story for Harper's Bazaar called "The Best Tressed List."

152

AMANDA BROOKS

Although Brooks is one of the most photographed New York socialites and the creative director of the Tuleh fashion house, her beauty mantra is "nothing fancy." "I wash my hair twice a week, and I get highlights only once a year," says the 28-year-old mother of one. **Favorite products:** John Frieda Sheer Blonde Moisture Infusing Shampoo ($6.50) and Frédéric Fekkai Moisturizing Shampoo and Conditioner with Shea Butter ($22.50 each). **Hairstylist:** Ricky Pannell at Snip N Sip (212-242-3880) in New York. **Colorist:** Alex Briones at Snip N Sip. **Secret trick:** After shampooing, Brooks rubs a dollop of Olay Active Hydrating Beauty Fluid ($6.99) through her hair. Then she pulls it into a knot and lets it dry naturally.

I FIRST discovered David Hicks when I was sitting in my mom's interior design office, age fourteen, browsing through her library. I picked up *David Hicks on Living—with Taste*, and then *David Hicks on Bathrooms*, and then *David Hicks on Kitchens*. The houses he designed were well within the bounds of good taste and classic design, but they also looked completely radical to me. His sense of color, his use of graphic lines and angles, his mix of antiques with modern furniture, his abundant and sophisticated combinations of print and texture, his strict, disciplined use of order and placement—it was as if he combined everything he

liked from every genre, resource, and era of design and put it together in a way that made total sense.

His style was intensely personal yet universally likable. He made things that on their own might seem hideous suddenly look beautiful when in the right context. For many years I studied all his books and tried to emulate his style in my own creative endeavors. My first stab at decorating our apartment on Chrystie Street (the one featured in *Vogue Living* on page 151) was directly inspired by my love of David Hicks, right down to the brown velvet and silver lamé upholstered X-bench I found at a thrift store in Palm Beach for $25. In the years since, I wouldn't be the only creative person inspired by him—Jonathan Adler and Tory Burch brought the David Hicks style into the mainstream with their own brands, inspired heavily by his genius. At first I was depressed to see this style I loved so dearly brought to the mass market, but if you look closely at his books, there is a lifetime of information to be had and endless ways to interpret it.

Above: Elliott Erwitt shooting India Hicks at David Hicks's house in Oxfordshire on a shoot I organized. I love the perfect symmetry of the garden.
Opposite: If there is one thing David Hicks is most known for, it's his brilliant and original print, pattern, and color mixes, all designed by him. This bedroom is classic David Hicks at his very best.

THOUGHTS ON TASTE

I don't particularly like the word *taste*.

Taste is safe. Taste is generic. Taste is bland.

Taste connotes an aesthetic that a vast many people find appealing. Why do we want to share the same taste as other people? Don't we want to have our own unique point of view?

The highest compliment someone could pay me might sound something like "I would never dream of wearing that, but it works on you." We are all human beings, alike in many ways but also vastly different from one another. Shouldn't our style reflect that?

These days when I use the word *taste*, I surround it with air quotes. Like when someone asks me if I like something, I might say, "Well, it's 'tasteful' but ultimately not that interesting."

Where I think taste comes in handy is when it's personalized and mixed in with someone's own style. I love a house that is a balance of things that would be considered tasteful and things that some people are skeptical of, maybe even calling them tacky.

The cruel part is that it's important to understand taste before you can subvert it. Taste is possible to learn, but what occurs beyond taste requires self-knowledge, a strong point of view, and a good dose of confidence.

"Good taste is something which you can acquire: you can teach it to yourself, but you must be deeply interested. It is in no way dependent upon money."

—David Hicks

156

This seventies room is a whole other side of David Hicks, but no less "him." I especially notice his balance of good taste with typically jarring colors here.

THE MET BALL CAN INDUCE THE HIGHEST HIGHS (A "WOW" FROM ANNA WINTOUR) AND THE LOWEST LOWS (ARRIVING IN A BEAT-UP MINIVAN)

THE MET BALL has always been the biggest sartorial opportunity of my year. I've taken complete and total pleasure in spending hours, days, weeks, even months contemplating my outfit and then spending even longer to (hopefully) make it happen. When it all comes together, there's no better feeling than walking into the fashion party of the year feeling confident. That said, sometimes the stars haven't aligned in my favor, and I've been left struggling at the last minute, desperately trying to add bells and whistles to a dress that just isn't working. Regardless of the success of my outfit, an invitation to the Met Ball induces tremendous excitement (Who will be the surprise performer? Which actress will I spy trying to fix her broken zipper in the bathroom? Who will be best dressed?) and utter insanity (What THE HELL am I gonna wear?). In the fashion world, there is no greater promise of high-fashion glamour, jaw-dropping celebrity sightings, and high-school-prom levels of anticipation than on this one night.

Opposite: A fitting at the Tuleh studio with pattern-maker Annika Paganakis for my ill-fated Met Ball look of 2004.

1997
The very first time I went to the Met Ball, I went as someone's date to the afterparty. We weren't invited for dinner, but it didn't matter

159

to me—I was just excited to be at an actual ball and have the chance to wear something fabulous. Being just twenty-three, I knew that whatever I could cobble together out of my mother's closet would be far better than anything I could afford to buy. Besides, my mother was over the moon that I'd reached the age at which it was finally appropriate to wear some of the things she had saved for me.

We played dress-up in her closet ("Hands off the Alaïa," I was quickly told) and eventually settled on a black silk floor-length fishtail skirt that Mom had bought at Vicky Tiel on a trip to Paris in the eighties. She then rummaged through her lingerie drawer and picked out a simple off-white silk camisole for me to wear on top. It was simple and chic but not breathtaking. We added her engagement ring from my father (having been divorced for twenty years, she had stowed it at the back of her jewelry box to be rediscovered one day). It was not a small diamond, but not quite enough to *make* the outfit. And then she ran back to her closet muttering something about "the shawls!" She came back with two duchesse silk shawls with generously frayed edges in the most beautiful pale baby pink and robin's-egg blue. I pointed to the pink, and she wrapped it around my shoulders and fastened it with an oversize knot at the front. That was it. It was elegant and glamorous, yet appropriately sweet for a young woman new to the city. The evening was okay—we got there late, it was crowded, everyone was a bit too drunk. But I'll always remember that night for the glamorous and grown-up feeling I had as I walked up the steps to the Met, red carpet and all.

2003

The first time I was invited to the Met Ball in its entirety, Tuleh designer Bryan Bradley was my date. I was working at Tuleh at the time and pregnant with my second child, Zachary. Anna Wintour and *Vogue* had recently taken over the event (having previously shared the duty on alternate years with *Harper's Bazaar*), and the evening already had the buzz of being bigger and more glamorous than ever. The theme was "Goddess," and Bryan made

me a white one-shoulder bias-cut silk jersey dress that fell elegantly over my growing belly. I did my own hair and makeup—braiding the front of my hair, fastening the back into a bun, and applying *lots* of smudgy black eyeliner. At dinner, Phoebe Philo and her husband-to-be, Max Wigram, were seated on one side of me. Phoebe was the Chloé designer at the time, and I was already in awe of her. She was shy, though. Max was an old friend of Christopher's, and so we found enough to politely discuss. On my other side was Karolina Kurkova, the supermodel, whom I had known since the earliest days of her modeling career. We had a hilarious time, mostly staring at people we were excited to see and bonding over the fact that neither of us was wearing any underwear because of the sheerness of our dresses! Diana Ross was the surprise musical guest, and we boogied until the party ended. Despite being five months pregnant and stone sober, the whole evening was a blast.

Arriving with designer Bryan Bradley in 2003, wearing a silk jersey Tuleh dress. My favorite maternity gown ever!

2004

The following year, I was still working at Tuleh, but Bryan was away at a trunk show, and this time *Vogue* invited me to attend with Christopher. The theme was "Les Liaisons Dangereuses." I was planning on wearing a ruched chiffon column gown in gray with small white polka dots. It wasn't really that on-theme, but it wasn't exactly off-theme, either. On the Thursday before the ball, Anna Wintour's office called. "Anna would like to know what you

161

It pains me to look at this picture, but here I am in my Tuleh dress in 2004 (next to Vogue's *then style editor Alexandra Kotur).*

are planning to wear to the Met on Monday," an assistant inquired. This is how things happen when you're in Anna's world; they come out of the blue and you don't ask questions. I described the gown and was told I'd get a call back shortly.

The phone rang again soon afterward. "Anna would like to know if there is something you could wear that is more in theme with this year's exhibition?"

"Sure!" I replied naively, just wanting to please. After all, I was surrounded by patternmakers and seamstresses in a studio that had made gowns in three hours, never mind three days. But the reality was that Bryan was halfway across the country on a plane, and there was no way to even get a sketch out of him until the following day at the earliest.

It was then explained to me by Anna's office that the *New York Times* Style section was looking to do a story on the process of getting dressed for the Met Ball. They were looking for a girl to photograph throughout the process of conceptualization, fitting, and then arriving on the evening in her custom gown. Anna recommended that I be the girl they follow, and the *Times* wanted to come photograph me at a fitting the next morning. I managed to get the shoot pushed back to the following afternoon and left a half dozen frantic voice mail messages for Bryan to call me the instant he landed.

After a harried few minutes discussing potential ideas, a simple idea dawned on Bryan. We'd done a show once using corsets, and he had a corset muslin lying around somewhere. It was natural

white cotton, so it would have to be dyed, and then we'd add layers and layers of floor-length tulle on the bottom to evoke the grandeur of nineteenth-century gowns. Annika, the patternmaker, and I found the corset and dug out as many yards of tulle as we could find. The look was promising. The photographer came to the Tuleh studio the next day and I stood on a pedestal in front of a floor-length mirror in the undyed corset and tulle skirt. It became a pretty picture, and the dress looked great.

God, how I wish we'd stopped fiddling with the dress then and there—the undoneness of the natural material was a good balance to the pomp and circumstance of the volume and proportion of the fitted bodice and giant skirt. But no. We didn't stop there. Late that afternoon, after the *New York Times* left, Annika and I decided we'd dye the whole thing pink. If it had been a very pale pink I think it would have been okay, but instead it was a more vivid purply pink. I looked like a Disney princess. If that wasn't enough, we then screen-printed it with graphic circular Tuleh logos that we'd had made for T-shirts and sweaters for our last runway show. We thought that the graphic element would add the modern edge the dress lacked. Once it was all done, I wasn't sure if I actually liked it.

But I did know the minute I put the dress on. It wasn't me. I curled my hair and put my makeup on (this was still before the days of being able to afford a hair and makeup team), waiting anxiously to feel that the look had come together. When there was nothing left to add, I surrendered to the reality that I'd show up at the Met Ball in a dress I didn't like. It wouldn't be the last time this happened but it was the first, and it was heartbreaking. To make matters worse, I was so concerned about my effing dress that I forgot to arrange a car to pick us up. And it was raining. I called every car service I knew and was turned down again and again. That left me with Delancey, which is the slightly squalid car service that picks you up at your door and costs only fractionally more than a cab. I'd begged them for a black town car, knowing full well that with Delancey, you can't really request a certain type of car—sometimes you get a perfectly respectable Lincoln Town

Car and other times you get something that has no resemblance to any kind of professional transportation. When Christopher and I arrived downstairs, with me already feeling dejected in my too costume-y dress, we were greeted by a beat-up burgundy minivan— yes, a minivan!—to take us to the Met Ball. As we pulled up, a sore burgundy thumb in a sea of sleek black town cars, our close friends and fellow downtowners Rachel Feinstein and John Currin were exiting the sleek black town car just in front of us. Thank God it was them. As fellow Delancey patrons, they doubled over in laughter at the sight of us, slightly terrified by the reality that it could easily have been them had Marc Jacobs, their host for the night, not arranged a more civilized car for them.

There is nothing more fun than the Met Ball when you're up for it, but it's basically a fashion parade in front of all your peers and colleagues. How can you feel good when you don't like what you're wearing? I do remember one moment that night—as I was walking to our table, both Renée Zellweger and Venus Williams came over to me to tell me how much they liked my dress. "You do?" I asked in disbelief before saying thank you. Most gracious people would be flattered, but I was too far gone about it at that point and wanted nothing more than to go home and take it off, which I eventually did. Being naked has never felt so good.

2005

The following year brought my personal favorite and, if I do say so myself, my chicest Met Ball look ever. The theme was "Chanel," my all-time most coveted fashion brand, and as I have a long-standing relationship with the PR girls there, I thought naturally, I would wear Chanel. *Naturally.* Although the fitting date was dangerously close to the day of the party, I felt confident I'd find something I loved. I walked into the second floor of the boutique with that adrenaline rush of expectation. *How am I going to choose between all the amazing gowns?* I thought before even laying eyes on the clothes.

On one side of the fitting room was a rack of beautiful and elegant ready-to-wear gowns, mostly in black and white. On the

other side were the couture pieces—my heart exploded with excitement until it dawned on me that they were the last few couture pieces on offer, the ones that hadn't been chosen as a first, second, or even third choice by the celebrities who were understandably invited to choose ahead of me. Don't get me wrong, there were some incredible things—richly embellished and intricately embroidered gowns, skirts, and jackets that would be amazing going down a runway. But it was obvious they just didn't translate into real life, or at least not into my real life, even if it was the Met Ball. So I went back to the rack of simpler clothes and found a stunning long black chiffon column gown trimmed in Chantilly lace with a satin bow falling over each shoulder. It's still one of my favorite dresses ever, but it wasn't right for the Met. First of all, every girl in fashion knows that Anna Wintour frowns upon black being worn to the Met; she wants everyone to look festive, and black clothes don't photograph well at night. Second, I feared it just wasn't *enough* for such a big occasion. It did fit beautifully, however, and at that point it was the front-runner.

My Chanel-inspired vintage look, with Chanel accessories, 2005.

I know, I thought, *I'll just jazz it up with accessories!* Chanel always has incredible accessories, and that season had more than ever. I picked out strappy black satin stiletto sandals with a giant (we're talking three inches in diameter!) faceted rhinestone covering the toes on each foot. The matching clutch was equally dazzling—it was a hard black rounded square with the same giant stone and smaller versions scattered around it. I'd add some flow-

ers to my hair and dramatic makeup. Although the outfit came home with me, I knew the minute I left the showroom that I wasn't convinced. I racked my brain for options and made a few phone calls looking for vintage Chanel from dealers and collector friends. "Too late," I was told unanimously. So I decided to have a look around my own closet. It only took a few seconds for my eye to land on a 1970s YSL sequin-and-feather bolero.

Several months earlier, my great friend Duro Olowu, a talented fashion designer and enthusiastic vintage collector (and featured on page 184), had hidden the YSL jacket in the back of his shop to save for someone special, and I coveted it so much that he had sweetly arranged a trade with my artist husband (the jacket in exchange for a painting) so that I could have it for my birthday. Ever since, I'd been waiting for the perfect moment to wear it. It wasn't Chanel, but it was certainly inspired by Chanel, and I figured I could pay homage to my favorite design house regardless of the brand I was wearing. The vision for the look came to me almost immediately: I would tone down the flashy and feminine YSL jacket and the over-the-top Chanel accessories with a simple white silk ribbed tank top and men's cut black crepe trousers. Yes, I would be wearing trousers to the Met Ball. And then to play up the black-and-white contrast, I'd wear a white gardenia in my hair with a black grosgrain ribbon tied around my bun.

I had another idea, but it was so out there that I thought I wouldn't decide on it until I was getting dressed the evening of the event. I'd seen a picture of Nicole Kidman months earlier wearing a flower corsage—yes, like for prom—on her wrist at a premiere. Something that had always seemed so tacky in my mind now looked so chic. I asked Lewis Miller, my go-to florist, to make up a gardenia corsage to match the one intended for my hair. I took one final risk and had my fingernails painted optic white. If it worked, my nails would add the slightest bit of irreverence to the classic chic of the rest of my look.

That night was one of those rare occasions when everything just came together as I'd imagined it—the balance of black and

white, the mix of masculine and feminine, the ode to Chanel with my own personal style mixed in. And it was the risks that made the look complete. I felt like a million bucks, and when I reached the receiving line, Anna Wintour looked at me and simply said, "Wow!" Certainly the best fashion compliment I'd ever received.

2006

That year the theme was "Anglomania," but to me that just meant wearing a British designer, and since I knew I wasn't going to get my hands on some amazing McQueen confection, I decided to ignore the inspiration that was given. I went to YSL for a fitting, having *loved* the previous runway collection, especially a black tulle cape with hot pink velvet roses embroidered on it. Despite having no idea what I'd wear underneath it, I felt dead set on wearing that cape. "It *should* be available," the design assistant assured me, "but I'll have to let you know tomorrow." So I waited optimistically until I got a phone call from YSL explaining that an actress had recently worn it for a magazine cover shoot, and she had a contract stipulating that no one else could wear it until the magazine came out on newsstands. (I'd later find out that the actress was Lindsay Lohan!)

So I got my second choice, which I still loved despite my disappointment at not having that incredible cape. It was a short black metallic tweed bubble skirt with tiny paillettes sewn onto it. The whole point of the skirt for me was that it had matching sparkly tweed suspenders. I *love* suspenders! It also had a giant purple taffeta bow sash that fastened around the waist. I didn't love the billowy chiffon blouse that the look was shown with on the runway—I thought the look needed one more masculine touch, not another feminine one. So once again I paired my Met Ball look with a silk tank top, this time in black.

I thought I would go for a Brigitte Bardot–esque, soft, feminine, sixties updo, so I went to a salon armed with a photo of the look I wanted. The hairdresser didn't really get it. He put a modern spin on the style, which left me looking kind of stiff and too up-

The suspenders were my favorite part of this YSL look, worn in 2006.

town. I went home and tried to fiddle with my hair, but there wasn't much to do. I left well enough alone and set off for the night.

Since the theme that year was celebrating English designers, *Vogue* had invited all sorts of British icons—actors, musicians, David Beckham—to attend. My husband, being English, nearly fell over when he got the chance to chat with David Bowie during cocktails.

As we approached our table with great anticipation about who our dinner partners would be, I went into a full-on panic when I saw who was seated next to me: Johnny Rotten. Of Sex Pistols fame. What the hell would I have to say to him? Especially with my bourgeois hairdo? My husband begged to switch seats with me (Johnny Rotten was a late seventies idol from Christopher's punk phase), and I would have been delighted to, but I knew that it wasn't worth the risk of offending our host.

Long after the rest of our table was seated, there was still an empty chair next to me. We all started our first course and placed bets on whether Johnny Rotten would show up. Eventually Anna herself led Johnny to his seat. He took one look at the table and then at me, and then turned to Anna and said—NO JOKE!—"I'm not fuckin' sittin' there!" The whole table looked at one another nervously, and then—what could we do?—we all started laughing, including Anna. She whispered something to him and then led him away and that was that: the end of my evening with Johnny Rotten.

168

2007

In 2007, Christopher and I were invited to the Met Ball by Tod's, the Italian accessories brand. With Tod's, as long as I wore their shoes and bag, I was free to choose my dress from wherever I wanted. I thought, *Who would I really love to wear?* I was finally feeling ready to wear a gown again, and it's hard to think of gowns without thinking of Oscar de la Renta. The theme was "Poiret," the great designer of the twenties, and while I'm a fan of his talent and its effect on the course of fashion, I knew I wasn't going to be too literal about it.

So I went up to Oscar's showroom and had a blast trying on nearly every long dress in the place. Eventually, I settled on a gown that was *completely* see-through black chiffon (yes, black despite the "no black" directive from Anna) on top, gathered and belted at the waist with a beautiful black ribbon, and then full volume on the bottom with very intricate and bold embellishment and embroidery. The shape of the dress wasn't exactly twenties, but the looseness and the intricate decoration were. I think I might have scared the PR team when I suggested I could just wear an opaque bra and hot pants under the dress. "Well," the head girl said cautiously, "I'm not sure that would be very *Oscar*." I got the message, and besides, she was right. The team at Oscar generously insisted on having their seamstresses line it with a delicate slip, thus saving me from running around having to find just the right thing to wear underneath. I was free to focus on getting the accessories right.

I set out doing styling research before going shopping, and I chose the eccen-

My Oscar de la Renta moment, with vintage Bulgari jewels, 2007.

tric Italian heiress Marchesa Casati as my early-twentieth-century muse. I loved her loose curls and her dark, black, smudgy eyes with a natural lip. With the black dress and dark eyes, the look was turning quite Goth, so I knew I also had to find something to lighten the whole thing up a bit. It was May, after all. I had often borrowed jewelry from Harry Winston but was told this year they didn't have enough insurance to cover me. I next called Fred Leighton and was declined there, too. So then I did what most girls in fashion do when they reach a dead end—they call *Vogue*. My savior—Meredith Melling, who at the time covered the entire fashion market—hooked me up with Bulgari, who, I was told, was pulling vintage pieces from their archives for the event. Now I was excited. After my initial jewelry heartbreak, I really struck gold with a vintage diamond necklace worth three million dollars that Madonna would wear to the Cannes Film Festival only weeks later. It was two strands of large round diamonds, and it added the perfect amount of "light" to the look. Now I just needed one more thing to balance it out.

Fresh flowers are my favorite go-to accessories for finishing an evening look. They are inexpensive and feminine, and you can guarantee no one else is going to have the same ones. So I called Lewis, my florist, and asked him what he had in white. He sent over a bunch of teeny-tiny miniature white roses, and immediately I knew exactly what I was going to do with them. I was going to have my hair curled quite tightly and then pin the flowers all around my head in between the flat crown on the top and the beginning of the curls. Was I nervous to take such a risk? YES. But I'd been around long enough to know that nothing great comes out of playing it safe—*especially* in fashion.

When the look came together, it was quite extreme. My eyes looked like a raccoon's and my hair was *really* curly. But I liked it. And I had to remember that in the evening, especially once you're inside the museum itself, the lighting is significantly dimmer than in my bathroom. I'd learned from experience that it's actually a good idea to go a bit heavier than I normally would on the hair and

makeup. I felt like myself in my clothes, on theme and just distinct enough from everyone else.

The night itself was a blast. J.Lo was at our front-row table and Jennifer Hudson, fresh off her Oscar win, sang the highlights from *Dreamgirls*, standing right above us. Boy, that girl can sing!

2008

Let me first say this. I *love* Marni. I love the prints, the florals, the furs, the nerdy version of chic, the unconventional proportions, and the exquisite colors. But the year I wore Marni to the Met Ball offered me another dose of fashion humility. It's tough to admit this, but my unsuccessful outfit was entirely my fault. I picked a great look, and I ruined it with the styling.

Marni was our host that year, so I went into the store a week before the Met Ball to choose a dress. The trouble was, they hadn't shown or created many formal dresses that season. There was one long gown, but it just didn't feel like me and the PR girl agreed. I went through nearly every look in the collection, and toward the end, a jade green skirt caught my eye. It was an odd length (mid-calf) and had a lot of volume, but I thought it was stunning, in a retro, fifties couture kind of way. To wear with it I wore a sheer, pale gray organza blouse that lay loosely over my shoulders and then billowed out in the back. It had absolutely nothing to do with the superheroes theme of the exhibition that year, but I loved it. It was romantic and pretty, which, truth be told, wasn't really my look at that time, but I was excited by the challenge to make something unfamiliar feel like me.

Mistake 1: I know now that I should have worn my hair loosely pinned back, in keeping with the soft femininity of the look, but instead I slicked it back into a bun, thinking I would create some sort of contrasting modernity. Not a success.

Mistake 2: I went to Seaman Schepps and borrowed a black onyx-and-diamond link bracelet that I wore as a necklace, tied around my neck with a black grosgrain ribbon, because the outfit wasn't quite dressy enough for the Met without it; I thought

My beautiful (if somewhat too casual) Marni blouse and skirt with bad styling by moi.

some heavy jewels would amp it up. I suppose it achieved its purpose, but it looked too weighty in pictures compared to the lightness of the blouse.

Mistake 3: I shouldn't have tried to make the look something it wasn't. I selected these sky-high satin platform sandals that I thought would give the look a bit of edge, but in the end they, too, just looked heavy. A good classic stiletto pump would have done the job just fine. The good news is that I wore the shoes over and over again after that night.

Despite my unsuccessful look, I had a blast. I had learned from my pink princess gown moment that life was too short to let my outfit ruin my night. After an early chat with American designer Phillip Lim, who knows me well enough to come up to me and say, "Amanda, that outfit is *so not you!*" we had a laugh and I got over myself. At dinner, Lou Doillon, the model/singer daughter of Jane Birkin and one of my all-time style icons, sat across from me in the gown I had stupidly declined (she made it her own by adding a beat-up leather jacket on top), and Robin Thicke sat at the end of the table with his then wife, Paula Patton. Meeting celebrities at the Met Ball is really fun because fashion is not their world, so they feel excited to be there and open to chatting. Also, everyone there assumes that everyone else is really important, so the atmosphere is very friendly.

2009

There was always a point every year when I wondered whether I would be invited to the Met Ball. Some years I was asked well in

advance, giving me loads of time to plan, prepare, and agonize over what to wear. Other years have cut it quite close.

Here's how it works: *Vogue* fills the majority of seats by asking big fashion- and beauty-related companies to buy entire tables. These tables go for hundreds of thousands of dollars. No joke. Then *Vogue* invites all the people who can actually afford the $25,000 individual tickets to send in their checks. I have never been one of those people. I have always been one of the girls that *Vogue* either sits at one of its own tables (as their guest) or I have been filler at a fashion brand table. After all, there are only so many celebrities you can sit together at one table before it explodes.

So in 2009, the invitation just never came. Not in the mail, not in an e-mail, not on the phone. Nothing. I waited and waited, and then I suffered through the "What are you wearing to the Met?" questions and the "Which afterparty are you going to?" queries and just figured that maybe my time was up. Maybe I wasn't the cool young fashion girl anymore. I was sad, but what could I do? I knew that most girls would kill to go to the Met Ball just once, and I had been going for many years.

My last-minute Phillip Lim dress, 2009. The shoes and bag are by Calvin Klein.

So on the day of the ball, Christopher and I resolved to do what any New Yorker does when at loose ends— eat sushi and go to the movies. Around ten thirty A.M. that day, I was at a graphic designer's office working on the layout of *I Love Your Style* when my cell phone rang. It was *Vogue*'s special events director, Stephanie Winston Wolkoff. Before I even finished saying hello she interrupted me.

"Do you have a dress for tonight?"

"Um . . . no, I don't have a dress for tonight. I haven't been invited."

173

"Well, get one—you and Christopher are coming."

And that was the end of the conversation. I nearly had the nerve to say that I needed to check with my husband first. Thank God she hung up before I could get the words out—I'm not sure she would have handled that so well.

After the initial shock of actually being invited to the Met Ball on *the day of*, I settled down for a minute or two until the insanity and panic set in. What would I wear? Who would do my hair and makeup? Would I be able to reserve a car? (I had learned from the minivan experience that a car for the Met Ball needed to be reserved days in advance.)

My first stroke of luck was getting Suzy Gerstein, my favorite makeup artist, to slot me in. She would have to come late, but she would be quick. And she would bring a friend to do my hair. I then called every single designer I knew and loved and asked them to send anything they had. The theme was "The Model As Muse," which pretty much meant anything goes in the outfit department. I didn't have much luck with the designers, though. Because *Vogue* dresses nearly every celebrity for the evening, all the designers had sent their best dresses over to the *Vogue* offices. When Suzy arrived at six P.M., I still didn't know what I was wearing. I had laid aside a magenta taffeta YSL blouse from the seventies from my own closet that I could have worn with a black column skirt, but I really wasn't that excited by it. A few options had arrived earlier in the day from various designers, but either they didn't fit or they were deemed not right for the evening. I had one final option on its way from Phillip Lim. He had promised me I'd like it. And when it finally arrived I did indeed. I loved it. It was so me. It was a short strapless dress covered in pale pink ostrich feathers and backed with gunmetal sequins. It was festive and fabulous and easy to wear. It was perfect.

Despite the humbling circumstances of the invitation, we were seated at a great *Vogue* table with Hamish Bowles, Alber Elbaz, and Marisa Berenson, whom I regularly cyberstalk for inspiration. Kanye West and Rihanna were the performers, and we danced and danced until everyone moved on to the afterparty at the Monkey

Bar. There I chatted with Tom Ford and met Madonna for a second time. Eventually, Christopher and I found our way to bed, exhausted from a day of last-minute panic.

2010

In stark contrast to the previous year, I was asked so early to the 2010 Met Ball that it was still actually 2009. The new special events director at *Vogue* was my friend Sylvana Ward Durrett. She is a fantastic girl with great style and a big heart. She called me in November 2009 to say that seats were already filling up for the following May, and she wanted to secure my and Christopher's places.

So now the question remaining was the perennial "What to wear?" The theme was "American Woman," not a big stretch for me. When thinking of a muse, I immediately thought of Lauren Hutton, who I wrote about on page 117. I did my research and had an idea of exactly what I wanted to wear. There was a picture of her in the seventies wearing gold lamé shorts and a matching gold lamé T-shirt with stiletto heels in the evening. Her hair was glossy and straight and, to me, in that moment, she was the epitome of American chic. You must be thinking, *Shorts and a T-shirt for evening??* I know. But I like the idea of reinventing formal evening wear, coming up with an imaginative way to dress for a ball other than wearing a gown. I knew I wouldn't find my ideal outfit on the runways so I went back to my friend Phillip Lim, hoping he'd think it would be fun to make this for me. He loved the idea.

I went to Phillip's studio and we looked at the pictures I had brought. He started pulling out his fabric bolts. Instead of a T-shirt and shorts, he suggested a jumpsuit. It would have a backless long-sleeved top, a set-in waistband, and then shorts on the bottom. I loved it. We both agreed it had to be shiny, and I was thinking maybe even sequins. Then Phillip left the room and came back with a bolt of khaki sequins. What could be more American than khaki and more glamorous than sequins? The combination was so good.

After the second fitting, the jumpsuit was perfection, and it was time to think about accessories. We looked through his col-

lection and I was immediately drawn to a very simple pair of nude suede pumps with an ankle strap. Phillip thought they were boring with the look. He wanted me to wear a stiletto sandal with a suede eyelet ruffle around the opening. I was sure it wasn't right. "How about I make it for you in nude suede to match the jumpsuit? It will be perfect," he said.

I went home with both shoes, convinced that I'd politely try his suggestion but then go ahead with the preferred simple pump. But when I had the outfit on with the glossy hair and the ever-so-slightly seventies makeup and one shoe on each foot, I realized that he was right. The ruffle shoe just looked better; it was less straightforward but more interesting. I left the house feeling confident and never reconsidered the whole night.

But the drama wasn't over. The hosts of the Met Ball are always uberfamous—George Clooney, Cate Blanchett, Kate Moss, Julia Roberts. And I always got a twinge of excitement walking up that long flight of stairs to the lobby knowing that I was about to shake the hand of someone I would never have the chance to meet in other circumstances. But this time it was different. The host was Oprah Winfrey!

I'd watched Oprah's show every single day that it was on for ten years. It would be waiting for me on my DVR every evening when I got home from work, and it would be the last thing I would do after working all day, arriving home to attention-seeking kids, and making conversation with my husband over dinner. *Oprah* was my salvation at the end of the day. I loved the variety—Julia Roberts talking about raising twins; Dr. Oz talking about the shape your poop should ideally be; Eckhart Tolle extolling the virtues of meditation; sister-wives explaining why sharing a husband worked for them. The show was easy to get into, compelling, entertaining, and often spiritually inspiring. Like millions of other people, I learned more about personal introspection, compassion, and forgiveness from *Oprah* than I did faithfully going to church every Sunday as a child!

I made Christopher skip the receiving line so that he could get a picture of me shaking Oprah's hand. When the chance arrived,

she was distracted and barely looked at me as I shook her hand and said, "I am so happy to meet you. I have watched your show for more than a decade, and I have learned so much from you." Just as Anna was giving me the move-it-along stare, and as my eyes left her to step forward, Oprah put her hand on my upper arm to get my attention back, and when I looked at her once more she said sincerely, "I am so glad to have been your teacher." That was all I needed. I gave it my best effort to make the moment matter, and I think it did.

Later in the evening I went up to my old friend Adam Glassman, who is now creative director of *O* magazine, and told him about my moment with Oprah. He said, "Well, did you get your picture with her?"

"Just one from the back that Christopher took."

"Well, come on, let's get a good one," he said, clutching my hand and leading me over to where Oprah was standing.

As he reintroduced me to Oprah, he told her I was a huge fan, and this time I got a hug! A hug from Oprah! It was as delicious and warm and comforting as I always imagined it would be. She said she remembered me from the receiving line by my khaki sequins. I guess the jumpsuit made more of an impression on her than my sincere words, but no matter. As we posed for the camera, she pulled me in tight to her and gave me another squeeze.

My custom-made Phillip Lim sequined jumpsuit, 2010.

As if the night couldn't have gotten any better, Lady Gaga was the musical guest, and I later got down with Phillip Lim at the afterparty, surrounded on the dance floor by Justin Timberlake, Jessica Biel, Pharrell, Oprah, and Anna Wintour. It was a perfect ending to a perfect night.

177

2011

My invitation to the 2011 Met Ball was another nail-biter. The show and gala were a tribute to Alexander McQueen, who had died that previous year. As I was newly ensconced in my role as fashion director for Barneys, I just assumed that I'd be going. In fact, I'd chosen my dress as I saw it go down the runway at the Giambattista Valli show in Paris three months before the ball. "That's the dress," I told myself, knowing full well that McQueen wouldn't be an option.

I knew I wouldn't be a freebie this year. *Vogue* would expect that Barneys would buy me a ticket, unless a designer wanted to have me as their guest. But days, weeks, and months passed and I heard nothing. I thought for sure someone would bring it up at some point. But no one did, and I was left to quietly wonder (once again!) if this year, in the biggest fashion job of my life, would be the year that I didn't go to the Met Ball.

And then the phone rang, just two weeks before the party. It was my friends at Tod's asking Christopher and me to join their table. The relief and the elation welled up as I realized that yet again, I'd be free to wear a dress of my choosing: I could wear the Giambattista dress! Well, I could if it was available. Of course you can't get an immediate answer from a designer when the Met Ball is concerned. I'm sure the team at Giambattista Valli had to check with every publicist under the sun to make absolutely sure that a celebrity didn't want to wear it. Eventually, I got my answer: The dress was mine.

This was a fairy-tale dress. It was a proper, formal, floor-length gown in white wool with black lace and jet bead appliqué. It also had a sixties-couture-inspired capelet that was attached on top that made it very of the fashion moment. It wasn't typical, and this is why I loved it unreservedly. I asked my friend Dana Lorenz, who designs Fallon jewelry, to custom-design a pair of glamorous yet ever-so-slightly hard-edged matching cuffs for my wrists. And I'd do dark, smoky eyes with stick-straight hair pulled back off my face to make the dress look more modern.

The whole look came together beautifully, and I had that always-craved-and-occasionally-achieved feeling of walking into the Met feeling like a million bucks. There was just one thing. The dress was heavy (it must have weighed forty pounds) and hot (two layers of wool crepe, in May!). I *just* made it through the night. There was no way I was going to any afterparties—I could feel sweat beads rolling down over my belly, and my shoulders were sore from holding up the weight of the dress. At eleven P.M., the night, despite being a great one, was clearly over for me.

One of my favorites, 2011. I knew the minute I saw this Giambattista Valli gown on the runway that I wanted to wear it to the Met Ball.

2012

I don't know if I'll ever go to the Met Ball again. I have put that part of my life aside for now. The last time I went, in 2012, was the first time I really wasn't expecting to go at all. I'd left Barneys and was on my way to England for a year off, and I felt that for sure I'd outgrown my *Vogue* freebie invite. But there I was at the Calvin Klein showroom to have a fitting for a New Museum benefit a few weeks before the Met, when my friend Nacole, who runs the PR department, asked me if I was going to the Schiaparelli/Prada-themed event.

"Well," I said, "I think this is the first year that I'm not gonna go. I haven't been asked."

"Are you kidding? You're coming with us," she said. I'd often gone to events as a guest of Calvin Klein (the company, not the person). The designer Francisco Costa is a longtime close friend, and I'd subsequently become friends with the people on his team as well. Going to a party with the Calvin posse was easy and fun. I knew it would be a cozy and low-key way to go to the Met, if such

Above: My final Met Ball look of my NYC years. Wearing Calvin Klein, 2012.

a thing were possible. I found a beautiful hunter green couture-inspired (again!) dress that had unusual yet sophisticated proportions. I wouldn't exactly call it Schiaparelli- or Prada-inspired but the couture details were certainly in step with the current trend in fashion.

The morning of the big day I woke up sick as a dog with a stinking cold. I forced myself to make the most of my last Met Ball (for a while, at least) before taking a break from New York. I wore my hair in a simple bun, did my own makeup, and debated a pair of black-and-white rhinestone post earrings. I decided against them and regretted it the minute I got into the car. I'd forgotten the "more is more" rule when it comes to the Met Ball. But what I regretted most was the snot running down from my nose for the entire car ride—I was sure it was red as Rudolph by the time I arrived.

I made it through the night and managed to have a good time despite eventually losing my voice completely. In a way, it was perfect. That night showed me loud and clear that I was ready for a break from this life where my sanity was dependent on whether I was invited to a party, and if so, what I was going to wear to it.

Opposite: I loved the back of my dress, although it was just slightly overshadowed by Lauren Santo Domingo's amazing Oscar de la Renta confection, 2012.

MATCHING MY LIPS TO MY NAILS

I OFTEN run into a dilemma in coordinating my lipstick with my nails. I don't wear nail polish that often, but when I do, it's always red. In summer I like a more orangy red, like Geranium from Essie, on my toes. In winter, I don't wear polish on my toes, but I do like a nice deep bluish red, like Fishnet Stockings, also from Essie, on my fingernails, just to lighten up the gloom a little bit. But here's the thing—I am a matchy person, one who likes to feel coordinated at all times. So if I am wearing red nails of any shade, regardless of whether it's on my toes or my fingers, my lipstick has to *exactly* match. No, not nearly match. *Exactly match.* This is no formulaic thing—because color, especially lipstick, looks different on everyone. So you have to find what works for you. After much searching and trial and error, I have found my matching red shades and I stick to them like religion. Red Square by NARS matches my summer red nail polish and Dragon Girl, also by NARS, matches my winter red. If, on the other hand, I don't want to wear red lipstick with my red nails, then I wear no lipstick. I focus on the eyes instead and wear a little extra eyeliner with my mascara and then just put Chapstick on my lips. I can't bear the idea of mismatched lips and nails. It's just a personal preference, and these little rules and disciplines we create for ourselves make life easier and help contribute to better knowing ourselves and our signature style.

Opposite: Filmmaker
Liz Goldwyn and dancer
Dita Von Teese matching
their lips to their nails,
2014.

DURO OLOWU

Handsome Duro, one of the best-dressed men I know. Opposite: Duro's world—his collection of furniture, textiles, art, sculpture, vintage clothing, and clothes he designs himself— is so inspiring that art dealer Jeanne Greenberg has given him two shows in her downtown Salon 94 galleries.

I FIRST met Duro in his shop on Ledbury Road in London back in 1997. He made exquisite women's clothes in vintage couture fabrics with heavy influence from his Nigerian heritage. Over the years I'd pop into his shop to see his new collection or take a peek at the extraordinary vintage finds he kept hidden behind the counter. Knowing I was an avid vintage collector myself, he'd play show-and-tell with all his latest finds—a rubber Balenciaga coat from the sixties, a mint Pierre Cardin jewelry set, a bolt of David Hicks fabric, a pair of floral brocade Delman shoes. Occasionally I'd scratch together enough cash to buy something from him; a snake waist belt with double buckles is a memorable favorite.

Besides being a wonderful and loyal friend who always asks after my husband and children before moving on to other topics, Duro has the most sophisticated taste of anyone I've ever met. He taught me to understand and appreciate African textiles and prints, so much so that I covered the tables with them at my wedding; encourages me to like things—jewelry, clothes, paintings—that I often don't understand until much later; and inspires me with his insistence on being true to one's self. He also has integrity, dignity, and self-respect. Whenever I have a big decision to make, whether about fashion, friends, or family, Duro is among the first I call.

MOLLY MILBANK

MOLLY WAS my stepfather Will's aunt, who spent many of her holidays with us. She always came impeccably coiffed and beautifully dressed, usually in a matching knit sweater and pleated skirt, with buckle-adorned pumps and sapphire-and-pearl-cluster earrings from Seaman Schepps that matched her blue eyes. But she never dressed in a way that would even hint at the many decades of important designer dresses, gowns, suits, and accessories that filled every single closet in her sizable home.

When I was twenty-seven, Will, who was in charge of Molly's finances, rang me up to announce that Molly had finally run out of her long-gone husband's fortune and that she would have to downsize to a much smaller apartment. He wondered if I could help her sort through her clothes. It was deemed early on that Molly's collection of clothes was so important that we first needed to call in the experts to offer anything collectible or historically relevant to the Met Costume Institute. Fashion historian Caroline Milbank, who happened to be Molly's niece, pulled out the Madame Grès gowns ("I made a tradition of buying one piece from Madame Grès each time I went to Paris," Molly once told me), the 1930s woolen skiwear, and a few Chanel pieces. Then I invited *Vogue* editor Hamish Bowles, who has one of the most comprehensive fashion collec-

tions in the world, to choose a few of Molly's things. Hamish said that what was so original about Molly's wardrobe was that she had major designer pieces from nearly every decade from 1930 to 1990. Most women had periods of their life when they bought fancy clothes, but Molly's passion for acquiring new things to wear spanned more than seventy years.

When Caroline and Hamish left, it was time for me to help Molly sort through what she would keep and what she would give away. Molly found it very, very difficult to let go of her clothes, despite having not worn the vast majority of them for decades. "I might wear that when I go to the beach next summer," she said as I showed her a pair of sandals, even though she hadn't ventured outside the city in more than ten years. She had a very isolated life. When I told her I lived downtown, she confided that she hadn't been below Forty-Second Street since the 1970s.

Even so, after Molly convinced me to put way more clothes in her "keep" pile than would fit in her new apartment, the leftovers in the freebie pile were still every girl's dream. Silk Lanvin gowns, knitted Missoni skirts and dresses, brightly colored Kenzo sweaters, a Chanel suit, a Giorgio di Sant'Angelo caftan, and countless Pucci separates all have a special place in my closet thanks to Molly, and I wear them regularly.

WHEN YOU ARE STUCK, ASK SOMEONE YOU ADMIRE WHAT THEY SEE FOR YOU

WHEN I THINK of my work in fashion thus far, I think of the wonderful jobs I have been lucky to have, the generous people who have mentored me, the incredible clothes I've worn, the inspiring places I've traveled to, the amazing parties I've been invited to, and the creative work that has given me so much satisfaction. I also think about all the guidance required to get me through those twenty amazing years. Sometimes I have sought wisdom from others in order to move on from a situation I didn't have my heart in anymore, or to figure out what I wanted next and how to get it. Other times I was trying to figure out how to deal with an employee who wasn't performing or ask for a raise from an employer. Sometimes I needed to stop and appreciate everything I already had. Whether by coincidence or design, my journey in fashion has been accompanied by an equally compelling journey to learn new ideas about myself, my life, my career, my family, and ultimately about how to be happy.

Opposite: DVF trying accessories on me for her runway show during the time I worked for her as a design consultant.

When I was twenty-four, I was at a friend's birthday party. It was the night before her actual birthday. When I asked her what she was doing the next day, her answer surprised me. She explained

that she was going to watch a demonstration of a woman having an hour-long orgasm.

"What?" I asked in disbelief.

Without an explanation, she simply replied, "Wanna come along with me?"

"Sure," I found my mouth responding, as if on autopilot. I don't know how to explain my spontaneous enthusiasm other than to say that my dad always taught me that life is an accumulation of experiences, and the more you have, the richer your life will be. So I guess somewhere along the way that got me in the habit of saying yes to new things.

The next day I went to the address my friend had given me. I can't imagine now why I didn't pick her up in a cab on the way, but for whatever reason I arrived there alone. And in advance of my friend. In fact, I was the first to show up. Yes, I am the girl who *always* arrives at an event early to get a good seat. So anyway, I walked in and plonked myself into the front row. Regena, the proprietress of this place called Mama Gena's School of Womanly Arts, intended to empower woman in all areas of their lives—career, relationships, sex, money, self-esteem. She loves to tell me now, seventeen years later, about the moment she first clocked me. Most women, she recalls, who showed up to the orgasm class had been to many of her classes before, working up the courage to attend the most controversial one of all. There were a few first-timers there, but they were well into their thirties, if not their forties. But there I was, Regena remembers, the youngest girl in the room by at least a decade. *And* I was in the front row. *And* I was wearing Chanel. Let me explain the Chanel. At the time I was working for Frédéric Fekkai, whose company was then owned by Chanel. This entitled me to the employee discount at the sample sale. I still remember the prices—shoes were $40, dresses were between $75 and $500 depending on the fabric and embellishment, bags were $150, and accessories like belts, jewelry, and sunglasses were all under $50. So yes, I was wearing Chanel, but it wasn't as expensive as it looked.

190

The class was thought-provoking. There was a woman of considerable age, easily in her late sixties, lying on a massage table on a small stage at the front of the room. Her husband manually stimulated her clitoris for just over an hour. He was moving his finger as if it was a remote control adjusting the intensity of her orgasm. He brought her up with the increased speed of his touch, and brought her back down with a slower one. She never had a grand finale climax—it was more like she was climbing hills—up and down, progressively getting higher each time until he felt like she had had enough. Even though it sounds overly intimate and even intrusive to watch this moment between a husband and his wife, it was more like watching a science experiment than it was like watching a romantic act that belonged in the bedroom. Let's just say I learned a lot that day.

I didn't have a reason to go back to Regena's school again until a couple of years later, when I felt like I needed some guidance in my relationship with Christopher. This time, I went to one class, and then another, and then yet another. I took classes on communication, flirtation, jealousy, negotiation, self-awareness, relationships, and ambition, among others. In fact, I did Regena's classes for nearly nine years, literally one after another. I learned about embracing the power of being a woman, about having fun no matter what, about asking people for things in a way that sounds appealing and not needy. I learned how to negotiate with my boss, with my husband, with my nanny, with my children. I learned not to compromise but instead to make room for multiple viewpoints and multiple solutions. I learned about resistance and how to recognize it and work around it. I learned to not be a martyr or a victim, to take responsibility for what I have in my life—the people, the things, the opportunities. And most of all, I learned how to figure out what I want. How to recognize what I want. How to get what I want. Well, at least some of the time.

One of the most valuable tools I learned from Regena was to ask people you admire what they see for you. It's such a simple concept, but it has proven so effective in my life. Here's the thinking: Often

it's much easier to dream big for someone you love and care about than it is to dream for yourself, so let your friends, mentors, colleagues, and even family members give their two cents. Knowing all they do about you, what is their vision of you being your best self, accomplishing your best work, and achieving your highest goals?

This strategy has served me very well in the best times and in the worst, but it was especially useful when I was at a crossroads with Tuleh in 2004. For the previous two years I'd felt that Tuleh would be my lifetime career. It was my dream job, and I felt so relieved to have the "defining" of my career behind me. But then so much about the job and the circumstances of the job changed, and I was unsure whether I wanted to further commit to the company by taking some equity or to get out altogether. Heeding Regena's advice, I went to see a lawyer, Betsy Pearce. She was and still is a fashion industry bigwig, having written contracts for Nicolas Ghesquière, Phoebe Philo, Alexander McQueen, and Christopher Bailey. I *so* did not feel entitled to ask her for help. But then a friend, fashion veteran Kate Betts, assured me that Betsy would be delighted to see me. I wrote her a polite e-mail, outlining what I wanted to discuss and asking very humbly if she would agree to meet with me. She wrote back immediately, and I was on my way to her office the next morning. We talked through both scenarios in detail, and she quickly pointed out that tying myself down to a declining company was not a great idea, and she felt I had more potential on my own than I did as a partner at Tuleh. I told her that my main resistance to that viewpoint was that I didn't have a clue what I would do next.

"Write a book," she answered simply and determinedly.

"Me? I'm not a writer. What would I write a book about?" I asked, feeling confused by her suggestion.

"Think of it as a branding exercise. You have worked for all these amazing people, but now it's time to tell the world who you are. What's your point of view on fashion and style?"

Betsy had planted a seed in my head that got me thinking. I liked her idea. But I just had no idea what I would write about.

I remember being at Art Basel in Miami with Christopher. We were sitting by the pool at the Raleigh Hotel, and my eyes were fixed on Donna Karan (who was standing at the bar), while brainstorming with Christopher about what kind of book I could write. And then a thought occurred to me. Years before, I had discovered *Cheap Chic*, a seventies manual/style guide celebrating personal style and dressing on a budget, written by Carol Troy and Caterine Milinaire. When I first flipped through this book, it had resonated with me so strongly. It depicted the scrappy way I had shopped all through my twenties, and it showed more individualism than I'd seen in present-day fashion. Right then I resolved that I would write a new version of *Cheap Chic* for today, including all styles and price points relevant now.

But how the hell was I going to write a book???? Sure, I'd written some pretty good essays and papers at Brown, but I certainly didn't feel that I could write an entire book. I spent a few months researching ghost writers—someone who could capture the essence of what I wanted to say and help me say it in a cohesive, identifiable way. I came across Tim Blanks, a fashion writer living in England, and once he agreed to meet with me, I flew to London to explain my ideas and see if he could help me articulate them in writing. I spent three days with Tim talking, talking, talking. I even wrote some things down for him. At the end of our time together, Tim turned to me and said, "You know what, love? You can write this book."

"Huh?" I wondered aloud while looking at him quizzically.

"*You* can write this book on your own," he reiterated. "You're a great talker. Just write the way you talk. Be conversational. Don't try to be a writer. Just write down what you would say to a friend."

Not believing a word he said, I asked him to move ahead with our plan for him to send me a writing sample. Sure enough, two weeks later a few pages summing up our work together arrived in my in-box. I dropped everything I was doing and sat down to read it. It was good. It was really good. But it didn't sound like me. I struggled to see how I could put my name on something that just

wasn't *me*. I was left with no choice but to take the confidence Tim had placed in me and start writing.

Armed with the challenge of having a new and exciting chapter to start, I left Tuleh. I would say that I was heartbroken, but in truth my heart had broken long before, when I realized that neither the success of the company nor the circumstances in which I was employed there had fulfilled my hopes and expectations. Shortly afterward, the universe gave my new direction a thumbs-up in the form of the woman who would become my mentor, Diane von Furstenberg.

The first time I laid eyes on DVF, I was caught in her bed, literally. It was 1993, and I was a freshman at Brown and had been dating her son, Alex, for a few months. We had come to New York for a weekend and were staying at her apartment. She'd been away and allowed Alex and me to stay in her place in the Carlyle. On Sunday afternoon, Alex and I were watching a movie in her bed, and he'd gotten up to get something in the kitchen. It was a cozy apartment and the entry door was directly across from her bedroom. When I realized that she'd walked in the front door, there was no time to vacate her room. In my family home, I wasn't even allowed to have a boy in my bedroom, let alone share a bed with one, and I was deeply embarrassed that she found me lounging around so casually in hers. My face was bright red. I apologized profusely, but she just laughed and told me to move over. She kicked off her high heels and crawled into bed next to me.

At the time, DVF was in the midst of figuring out the next steps toward relaunching her brand, having closed her fashion business many years earlier. Diane has often said that it was a vulnerable time in her life, but from my point of view, she was empowered and confident and had a very seductive way about her.

I'm not sure what DVF saw in me when we first met. I was wholesome, "not the beauty I would grow into," as she likes to tell me, and probably a bit overly enthusiastic. But she included me in her creative process, asking what I thought of the book she was about

to publish or the line of knitwear she would soon sell to millions of women on QVC. Her mission was to create environments, clothing, and relationships that encouraged women to feel good about themselves. That first stage of our relationship didn't last long, as Alex and I soon parted ways, but she left me with a sense of approval and self-esteem that ushered me through my college years.

Years later, after I graduated from Brown and moved to New York, Diane and I encountered each other again. Each time I saw her I felt that same connection, that closeness I had felt to her for that brief time when I was in college. Again, she took an interest in me and paid me more attention than I would have expected. Our relationship progressed from seeing her at parties to being invited to events at her home or studio, and eventually she and I would have lunch together, just the two of us. The first time this happened was just after I left Tuleh. DVF invited me to have lunch with her in her West Village town house. I was nervous and not nervous at the same time. I was humbled by the attention and felt so lucky, but also felt the pressure to present my best self and not be boring!

We chatted and chatted over lunch and then when the conversation lulled, she said, "So! You are at a turning point in your career, darling. I think it is time you do something on your own. You have had some impressive jobs working for very successful people, and now it's time that you find your own success. You have the talent, the intelligence, and the experience to create something in your own vision." I told her I was in the midst of writing *I Love Your Style*, and she loved that as a first step. When I left that day she gave me a gift, an African hand-carved wooden bowl with a zebra pattern painted on it, to mark this occasion of renewed independence in my life.

After soaking up every ounce of wisdom offered by Regena, Betsy, and DVF, I gave myself a self-help break for a while, until yet again I found myself looking for answers. I heard from a friend about a business coach named Mark Flashen, who was very effective in helping people achieve their career goals. I was in transition at the time—I'd left Tuleh, was nearing the end of writing *I Love Your Style*, and

was trying to figure out my next career step. I had recently taken on the role of contributing editor at *Men's Vogue* and was writing a blog called *In Her Eyes*, which was a blend of street-style photos, vintage photographs, and writing, all commenting on men's style from a woman's perspective. It was really fun—I loved it, in fact—but it only took up a half day per week maximum and I was looking for more to fill my time and my bank account. I wanted to embrace the diversity of the jobs on my résumé and leverage the experience I had and the connections I had made. Mark got me thinking about starting a consulting company. "Consulting on what?" I asked. I wasn't sure of anything I was doing in my work life at that stage, and I felt stagnant. The first thing Mark did was hold me accountable to things I said I would do or wanted to do. He gave me homework—call this person, e-mail that person, write this list, record your thoughts.

Mark taught me about setting a goal and holding that goal in your mind, but not worrying too much about how to get there. He likened it to sailing: You set a point on the horizon where you want to end up. In order to get there by sailboat, you have to zigzag, and the wind or the current might blow you off course, but eventually if you keep the destination in your sights you will get there, even if your course is not a straight line. This idea stayed with me, and I still think about it all the time. The destination I chose back then was to be a champion of designers, to encourage them, to promote them, to help them accomplish their goals. I was tired of working with just one brand at a time. I loved the personal relationships I had with a handful of young designers, and I wanted to find a way to turn that into a job. The first step in that goal was becoming a fashion consultant. Mark made me establish myself as a company, Amanda Brooks Inc., before I had even one client. Kind of like "If you build it, they will come." And they did. Anna Wintour e-mailed me shortly after and asked if I wanted to help out Liz Claiborne. They were trying to realign their image as a fashion-relevant brand, and she thought I would be a good person to help them. It wasn't the coolest first client to have, but there was a great day rate involved and I knew I had the tools to be effective there. Then Diane von Furstenberg

followed. She wanted me to be a design consultant, bringing my taste and experience and personal point of view to her design team. Working for DVF was a dream, most of all because I got to watch her in action—how she freely expressed her point of view, how effectively she communicated with her staff, and how gracefully she balanced being a designer *and* the president of the Council of Fashion Designers of America with being a wife, mother, and grandmother. I had known DVF in a personal way for many years, but seeing her work only multiplied my admiration of her.

I did similar work for Tory Burch; looking over her collection, suggesting which pieces might be added, bringing in vintage samples or old photographs for inspiration. Next came Revlon. Like Liz Claiborne, Revlon wanted to bring back the aspiration to their brand, and I would show them how to use fashion to that effect. Under my recommendation and guidance, they hired current creative director Gucci Westman and sponsored many young designers' shows. Similar work then came from American Express. I helped them bring access to the most exclusive fashion brands, such as Alexander Wang and Proenza Schouler, to their cardmembers. I loved how this work felt so beneficial to both the big corporations with the deep pockets and the young designers who so valued their support. I also loved the feeling that all my previous job experiences had led me to this place and were now informing the work I was doing. These consulting opportunities proved successful enough that William Morris Endeavor hired me full time as their in-house fashion director, to both represent fashion designers and also to guide big corporations looking to benefit from their consumers' love of those designers and the clothes they designed. I never thought I'd be working at a Hollywood entertainment agency, but I was doing work that I enjoyed, and at the same time getting closer to the point on the horizon I had chosen as my destination.

A year later, when Barneys was looking for a fashion director, they called me. I immediately wondered if this was to be the destination on the horizon that I had unwittingly yet faithfully chosen a few years before with Mark Flashen.

197

RULES FOR CONSULTING

At twenty-five, I earned my first role as a consultant. I say "earned" because consulting is a privilege you are rewarded with through hard work and experience. You need to know how the fashion industry works, who the players are (and preferably have their phone numbers), and have a well-developed point of view before you are able to contribute creatively, intellectually, logistically, financially, or strategically to a brand. When you have reached the position of being able to use your knowledge and expertise, here's how you get started:

HOW TO KNOW WHAT YOUR RATE SHOULD BE
Whenever I ponder how much I should be paid for a given job, it's amazing how often I come back to the very first number that pops into my head. Of course I find it difficult to trust only myself, so I usually talk it through with my husband, a colleague in the industry, and my lawyer before I trust my own initial instinct, but it's usually my gut that leads me to the right number. And why shouldn't it? At this point I've had years of experience in negotiating and lots of advice from trusted sources. But how do you begin? How do you establish your initial day rate?

—First, ask around. Find out what others in positions such as yours are being paid for similar roles. Various lawyers I employed on my behalf over the years were most helpful in this regard. And also through paying attention to what freelancers were paid in various companies where I worked, I had a sense of who to compare myself to.

—What are the terms? Are they guaranteeing you a certain number of days each week, month, or year? The more of a commitment of time they give you, the more of a discount you should give them off your top rate. The value of this, though, is that you have the security of knowing that you have X number of days already paid for in that time. Conversely, these people are not employing you full time and you are not receiving the benefits of health insurance, pension, or Social Security from them, so your rate should certainly be higher than a full-time employee in a similar position.

—You also have to raise the number from what you actually want to receive to leave room for them to feel as if they are in control. Only very occasionally do people pay you what you ask for. When they do it's a great feeling, but always be prepared for them to knock your rate down a bit.

—Then, you have to see how the number that makes most intellectual sense sits with you on a personal level. If you feel perfectly comfortable asking for your day rate, then it is certainly too low. I like to feel intellectually justified but also slightly scared to ask for any amount of money in exchange for my services. Negotiating isn't ever comfortable.

—Always negotiate on behalf of yourself. Your employer is likely to give you more (it's easier to beat up a lawyer or agent than it is your future employee), and it's good for your confidence and your business skills.

LOGISTICS

In order to have a well-functioning freelance work life that maximizes your time effectively, you need to establish some rules with your employer. Now, I can't say these rules would necessarily fly if you are twenty-two years old and just starting out, but by the time I was thirty, had worked for a handful of impressive companies, and was running my own consulting company, these rules were imperative to ensuring that my time

was used in the most effective manner.

—The minute you leave your office to go to an outside meeting on behalf of a client, you charge three hours, the equivalent of half a day. Think about it—you need to get yourself to the meeting, have the meeting, and get to wherever you are going next. By most city standards, it's quite possible that it could take you forty-five minutes or an hour to get from one meeting to the next, making it impossible to fit another client into your half day, so you should bill your client for that time.

—For the same reasons as above, as soon as you spend more than four hours at any client's office or at a meeting on their behalf that is away

199

from your office, you charge a full day's rate.

—Whenever possible, avoid charging by the hour, even for work done in your own office on a client's behalf. Keeping track of hours is tedious and takes time away from creative and strategic thinking. It's far better to put some thought into how many hours a project will take and get the client to agree to those hours in advance. Apart from meeting time, I always have research and presentation hours built into my contracts and negotiated in advance. You may not get the hours perfectly right the very first time, but you will learn quickly. Also, you can have an agreement regarding additional hours if need be. Occasionally, if I found I

was working longer hours on a project than was agreed to, I notify the client and they have the choice of committing to more hours from me or not.

HAPPINESS IN CONSULTING

—I have never found the one perfect consulting client, nor do I ever expect to. The gratification that I found as a consultant came from my work and my clients as a whole, on the balance, more than it came from any one person or company. There are so many ways to be unhappy or annoyed as a consultant—the client doesn't listen to you, they don't follow through on what you suggest, they changed your idea, they took credit for your idea, they don't use you as much as you

thought they would—it goes on and on. But here's the thing—you must not define yourself or your happiness through any one client. However, when you gather and select clients and add them to your stable, consider how they will fit in to the whole picture: Do you like what the company does? Are you proud to work for them? Do they pay well? Is it a reasonable commitment of time? All of these things are relative to what your working life looks like now and how you can improve it.

—The cool factor of your clients. This is another aspect of consulting that works on the balance. No one expects all your clients to be cool, not even in the fashion industry where everyone is ultra self-conscious about

appearances. It is usually the uncool ones that pay the most, either because they are very big companies or because they desperately need help. It is often those jobs that make it possible for you to work for smaller, cooler companies that pay you a fraction of the amount but deliver a different kind of satisfaction. Some of my most meaningful work experiences as a consultant came from working for small, start-up designers who paid me in clothes or jewelry for my services.

MAKING TIME FOR YOUR OWN CREATIVITY
—The final key to happiness through consulting is having a project that is just yours. When I first started Amanda Brooks Inc., I was still writing *I Love Your Style*. I thought it would be really difficult to manage both at the same time, but I quickly learned how much I valued carving time out of my day to indulge my own point of view. It also helped my relationship with my clients because it took the pressure off trying to satisfy my creativity through the work I did for them. I was able to be more objective and less attached to the outcome. When I finished *I Love Your Style*, I immediately felt the hole that project left in my work life. So I started a blog. Your own project can be anything—my friend Taylor runs a flower-arranging business in between the work she does for her fashion clients—as long as you find even just an hour a day to indulge your own instincts and flex your own creative muscle.

I HAVE ALWAYS SPENT TOO MUCH MONEY ON CLOTHES . . . AND IT HAS ALWAYS BEEN WORTH IT (UNTIL IT WASN'T)

IN 2005, I was thirty-one years old with two children. I worked at home, writing *I Love Your Style* and running my consulting company, and I had financial priorities beyond spending all my money on clothes; I had kids with future college educations to save for and a larger apartment to maintain. Inspired by an increased sense of self-knowledge and a growing focus on practicality, my clothes were still fashionable, but they were far more casual and timeless. I resorted to carrying an old Hogan "fishing bag" that went with everything (gone were the days of changing my purse every day to match my outfit), and it had a cross-body strap so that I could be hands-free to push a stroller or hold a child's hand. I also bought three sets of Phillip Lim cashmere track suit pants and matching cardigans that could be worn with slippers at home or ballet flats to pick up the kids from school.

Opposite: Heading to a fashion show in the new Alaïa skirt and shoes and Céline sunglasses I bought at Barneys with my mother's vintage Sonia Rykiel lace top.

Around that time, *Harper's Bazaar* called to interview me for a regular column called "Dressing for Your Age," which prompted me to think more specifically about balancing real life and fashion. I told them that I hated the word *appropriate* (overused during my upbringing) because I believe that if you love what you wear and it

203

suits you, who cares what anyone else thinks? Nan Kempner in a crop top at age seventy-two comes to mind. That said, my style had started to gravitate toward a more classic and understated look, because (A) I felt most like myself when not overshadowed by what I was wearing, (B) it worked well in my lifestyle, and (C) as I reprioritized my finances, I wanted to buy things that wouldn't go out of style next season.

As I settled into my thirties, I also borrowed less clothing from designers and dug into my closet for evening pieces handed down from my mother, or things I'd bought years before and had put away for another day. My best rediscovery was a floor-length dress that I'd bought at the Alaïa outlet in my early twenties, when not many people were wearing his clothes. With his return to big-time relevance in the mid-2000s, that red dress, worn with my mom's vintage teal Alaïa belt, was suddenly the chicest thing. My picture made it into the papers far more often for wearing original things that actually belonged to me rather than borrowed fashions du jour.

Just as I was moving away from an obsession with having the latest thing, I landed the job as fashion director at Barneys, and everything I had learned up until that point about investing wisely in fashion went straight out the window.

We can all relate to the feeling of overspending on clothes, can't we? You're standing there in a store in front of something you feel you *have* to *have*, and suddenly your entire future hinges on the boyfriend you're going to get if you wear this out tonight, or the job you'll get if you wear that to the interview. And in many cases, it's true, it does. Clothes have an awesome ability to empower us to be who we want to be or to convince others of who we are. They allow us to be flexible, too. By day we can be a serious business-woman; by night, we can transform into a sexy seductress. Or we can change from bohemian goddess to sleek minimalist from one day to the next, depending on what our lives require from us.

Spending money on clothes is relative, though. When I was in my early twenties and my parents were still helping me with my rent, spending irresponsibly meant buying two pairs of trousers

instead of one at Zara, or going back to the ATM at the flea market when I'd already spent the $100 I'd budgeted for myself that day. As I got older, spending irresponsibly meant ordering too much at a designer's showroom so soon after their runway show that the intoxication of newness had yet to wear off. I justified it by telling myself that since I was only paying wholesale, I didn't need to pay too much attention to how much I was ordering. That resulted in some painful surprises. Eventually, overspending on clothes meant making impulse handbag purchases at Céline when I was traveling in Europe. Spending money while away from home is like eating dessert off someone else's plate—somehow it feels like it doesn't count.

Although this may sound indulgent, even reckless, it actually paid off in spades. The way you express yourself through your clothes is what the fashion industry is all about. A first impression is the only one that counts, and I was determined to make sure mine was a loud, clear statement.

But then, one day, I came to the end of this glamorous near-fantasy. In the year I worked at Barneys, I spent *way* too much money on clothes, period. And it led nowhere. Unlike many other high-profile fashion jobs, being a fashion director didn't come with a clothes allowance. In fact, it came with a discount that was even smaller than the one I already got directly from the designers. And yet I was expected to represent the store and the designers it sold through my outfits. A fun challenge? Absolutely! However, it was new territory. As much as I've always loved buying and wearing clothes, I'd never paid much attention to what season my clothes were from or how many times I'd worn something as long as the final result felt like "me." I was also aware of the temptation that would arise being surrounded by the most incredible clothes in the world throughout my day, and I quickly surrendered to the fact that I was going to spend *a lot* of money at Barneys. I resolved, however, that I was going to do it wisely. I embraced brands like Céline, Derek Lam, Azzedine Alaïa, and The Row that are known for including beautiful classic basics in their collections—clothes that are of

designer caliber but don't scream "look at me!" (okay, maybe Alaïa screams "look at me," but still, it's timeless) or get pushed to the back of your closet after just one season. I also discovered less season-specific pieces in the commercial collections of my favorite trendy brands like Proenza Schouler, Thakoon, and Phillip Lim. Despite my investments being wise, all this shopping quickly burned a hole in my wallet, and it just didn't feel right. I was making more money than I ever had in my life, and what did I have to show for it? While I now have a closet full of beautiful designer clothes that will last decades, if not a lifetime, it took me a year to pay off the debt that resulted from overspending at Barneys. Ouch.

I was so excited to carry this Phillip Lim bag to the shows in Europe. He gave me the very first sample so I had it before anyone else, and it went on to become a big hit. The Lanvin shoes were bought with the justification that I was investing in my fashion week comfort.

HOW TO RECYCLE TRENDS AND MAKE
ICONIC PIECES LAST A LIFETIME

WHETHER I am living out of one humbly sized closet (as I am now) or two large walk-in ones (as I did in New York), it's important that I have a system of managing my clothes. My relationship with clothes is always a cyclical one—sometimes ruled by season, sometimes by trend, sometimes by practicality, but always by attraction. How excited I am by an item of clothing at a given time dictates where it resides within the visual space of my closet, or whether it even deserves a space in my closet at that moment. Twice a year, I reorganize my closet. I pick my favorite or most useful things and arrange them by item. More impactful items like jackets, blouses, and dresses tend to take center stage while trousers and skirts seem to always end up on the periphery. Anything that is blatantly out of season either gets put in moth-proof wicker baskets under the bed or in boxes in the barn until the weather changes again. Brand-new things are always front and center, regardless of the season.

Then there is fashion purgatory. When I come across an item of clothing that I don't think I'll wear anytime soon—perhaps I've grown tired of it, haven't worn it as much as I expected to, or wore the hell out of it but it's a trend that I am ready for a break from—the item gets removed from my closet, and put in a trunk and stored for a longer duration. Three things can happen to an article of clothing that gets put in purgatory. In the first scenario, I'll suddenly think of a given item because (A) I've missed it, (B) I suddenly have a use for it, or (C) it's become relevant again. In any of those cases I dig it out from its hiding place, it comes back to my closet, and I'm relieved I hadn't gotten rid of it. The second option happens when I don't think about an item at all and know that I'm unlikely to ever wear it again, but feel I can't get rid of it because it means something to me—such as my most important Tuleh pieces, anything by Chanel, anything that belonged to my mother, or maybe just something that I think is iconic or my daughter might like to wear someday. At that stage there are also the items that are ready for a permanent visit to the thrift store, usually things that weren't too expensive or I just feel are not significant enough to take up space in storage. Those things are banished forever!

Of course, this selection process has resulted in some regrets from time to time. Just the other day I was thinking of my scrunchie collection from the nineties. I was, and still am, 100 percent sure that a scrunchie was neve

going to make its way onto my head again. But now my thirteen-year-old daughter loves them. When she first asked me for one, I went into shock and wondered out loud if there was a support group for moms whose daughters want to wear a scrunchie. But now I've gotten used to the sight of them holding her ponytail up high on her head, and I wish I'd saved mine to pass on to her. I also miss my Marc by Marc Jacobs military-style denim jacket. It would have been so useful to wear on the farm. I guess I wore it until I was so sick of it that I thought I'd never wear it again. But now it seems fresh to me, and I miss it.

I've also had great successes in reincarnating items and giving them a second or even third life. One of my most prized fashion possessions is a black velvet Oscar de la Renta jacket with gold embroidery arranged in a baroque pattern all over it. It's a big statement. It had belonged to my mother in the eighties—I remember she wore it to a New Year's Eve party in Palm Beach and then again to the opera in New York. When I was old enough to carry it off (my late twenties), my mother handed it down to me, and despite how elaborate and ornate it is, I've gotten a lot of use out of it in the last decade. We all think that it's the simple things that become classic, but sometimes something over the top can be just as consistently chic. I've worn that jacket to a Tom Ford dinner, a Christmas-caroling party in Brooklyn, a Carolina Herrera book signing, and another Christmas cocktail party in England. And I've worn it with everything from a floor-length silk skirt to ripped jeans and sneakers. In my closet it's gone from front and center to purgatory and back many times. In fact, once someone from Oscar de la Renta's design team saw me wearing it in a magazine, and the next day I got a call from Oscar's office to say that he would love to have that jacket for his archive. They offered me anything I wanted from his store to trade for the jacket. What a dream! I went in so full of promise and excitement, tried on everything, found a few stunning dresses, but in the end I couldn't commit to the deal. The thing I knew about my jacket was that I had loved it consistently for more than two decades. I had probably worn it once a year for the past six years. It was too hard to know *in advance* if I was going to love any of these new pieces as much and for as long. Thank God I kept the jacket. I am grateful for its stunning and original design, its longevity in my closet, and the fact that it came from my mother. When it comes to the emotional attachment we all have to clothes, some things are just not replaceable.

Opposite: Mom, with my stepdad, William, in her embroidered velvet Oscar de la Renta jacket, 1980s. Left: Me, with Carolina Herrera at her book launch at Bergdorf Goodman, in the hand-me-down from my mom, 2004.

CAMILLA NICKERSON

IF I HAD to nominate the best-dressed woman in the world, Camilla Nickerson would be my choice. I met her early on in my time in New York (she is an old friend of my husband's) and then I had the privilege of seeing her at the school run every morning for seven years (where we both had kids). When I tell you that there was not one day that I saw her when her outfit wasn't perfect and inspiring, I'm not exaggerating. And when I say perfect, I don't mean perfect as in groomed and polished. I mean perfectly disheveled, or perfectly ironic, or perfectly proportioned. She just has an instinct for combining something classic with something unexpected. She makes you think twice. Once I ran into her at the movies and she was wearing a couture-shaped tweed jacket, flared jeans, black leather hiking boots with electric blue laces, and a Chanel bag. She looked so chic, but casual enough that she didn't look silly at the movies. No wonder Phoebe Philo (at Céline), Sarah Burton (at Alexander McQueen), and Francisco Costa (at Calvin Klein) all rely on her to style their shows.

Opposite: It's not just Camilla's amazing clothes that make her style so coveted; it's the original way that she wears them.

212

"ALL WOMEN NEED A GOOD DOSE OF HUMILITY FROM TIME TO TIME."
—DVF

THERE HAVE BEEN three times in my life when I have effectively cut off all my hair. The first was when I was eleven. At that age I had no idea how lucky I was to have long, thick, naturally blond hair. All I cared about was that it had been the same for way too long. Because it was the eighties, I had begged my mom for layers—like, serious eighties-style layers. Uhhhhhhhh, no. She wasn't having that. Getting wispy bangs was the closest I came to an eighties 'do. Then I wanted to dye my hair, as my older sister had been allowed to do, turning hers a perfect Molly Ringwald pinkish red. "Wait until you're thirteen" was the response that quashed that ambition. But then I finally got a yes. I was obsessed with the movie *Some Kind of Wonderful*, and I decided I wanted to look just like Mary Stuart Masterson's character in the movie. It was a boy's haircut, in effect, but it was blond enough and just long enough in the front to maintain some femininity. So in I went to Studio One—our local hip (in a suburban kinda way) hairdresser—and showed the lady a picture of the look I was going for.

My best friend's mother, Viveka, was the only one who was honest with me about my new look. "Darling, what have you done?

Opposite: At the Chanel book launch for I Love Your Style *with my freshly cut hair. Over the course of the week, I'd cut off a foot and I was loving it at this length.*

215

Your hair looks horrible!" I guess I'd known it did, but I wasn't able to admit it to myself until that moment. When the lady had cut off my hair, all the years of natural blond highlights went with it and the result was a poor man's version of "Watts's" look—a mousy brown mop of hair that was way too thick for such a short cut. But still, I was young enough to not really care about how I looked, and I was still feeling the triumph of convincing my mom to let me do something radical.

It took two years of awkward in-between styles to grow my hair back to its normal length, and once I could recognize myself again, I would keep it that way—falling just below my boobs—all through high school and college. Around the time of my graduation from Brown, my mom said to me one day, "Sweetheart, I think it's time you cut your hair shorter. Such long hair is really more becoming on very young girls." "You're right," I said, without much thought. "I should."

Weeks later, when I returned to my usual summer job working for Patrick Demarchelier, I had a new look. Once again I had cut my long, bohemian, wavy hair, but this time into a neat, shoulder-length bob. Again, I wasn't too sure about the result—I was worried I looked like a soccer mom—and my doubts were confirmed when Patrick caught a glimpse of my new look and said in his very heavy French accent, "What deed you do vis your 'air, darling?" He then called over Patrick Melville, the on-set hairdresser, and said, "Do somesing vis her 'air." So Patrick M. started cutting, in BIG chunks. I don't know what came over me. I just let it happen. Did I not care? Did I not have the confidence to ask him what he was doing before he started cutting? Before I had a conscious thought, I had a Jean Seberg pixie cut. I was numb the rest of the day. I went home that night and cried and cried. My mom cried with me, and my always loving and supportive stepdad couldn't help but comment that I looked like a cancer patient. I think he was upset because I was so upset. I knew it was just a haircut, but it was traumatic, and it zapped my already fragile just-out-of-college self-esteem.

I quickly figured out that I would have to reinvent my whole look to go along with my new haircut. Earrings of any kind would not work, but it was imperative that I wear mascara every day. My tomboy clothes were suddenly too masculine without the contrast of my long, wavy hair, but overtly feminine clothes just made me look like a girl who chopped off her hair. Luckily, I was headed off to Europe for two months on a graduation trip from my parents, which would buy me time to figure out my new look and let my hair grow in a bit before debuting myself as a job candidate in the real world.

It would end up being another two years before I really felt like myself, yet again. The irony is, I look back now at the pictures from those years and think I looked pretty cute.

The drastic pixie cut I endured at age twenty-two.

I'm sure most women can relate to going for a dramatic new haircut and being horrified with the result. I wonder, why do we do this? Are we looking for a new identity? Or to shake ourselves out of a rut? Is it boredom? What is it?

217

I think I found the answer, at least for myself, the third time I cut my hair short. My hair had now been back to my signature long, messy, boho waves for more than a decade, during which I had stuck with the same hairdresser—a former assistant of Orlando Pita's named Ricky Pannell who had an adorable salon called Snip N Sip in the West Village. The salon was filled with kitschy beauty-salon-related memorabilia from flea markets and featured an old soda fountain surrounded by glass jars of candy and chocolates. Ricky charged $95 for a haircut, a relative bargain by New York standards. Also, he had high-fashion experience and taste, but his belief was in giving women classic, easy, low-maintenance haircuts and saving the fashion statements for the styling. Perfect for me. Shortly after having my first haircut with him I was asked by *Harper's Bazaar* to be featured in a story called "The Best Tressed List." I was incredibly flattered, and even more excited when I learned the photographer was Francesco Scavullo, one of my photography heroes. The result was the closest I will ever look to a *Cosmopolitan* cover girl (not that it's exactly a look I aspire to). I had a slightly flirty look on my face, and I have to say my hair—having had a lot of effort put into making it looking "effortlessly" wavy—looked damn good. I credited Ricky with my haircut, and thus began the endless stream of women marching to Ricky's salon to get the same look. I was even in the salon on a few occasions when these women came in. Ricky, of course, was delighted (he never charged me for a haircut again), but he always laughed when women came in with my photo, and said, "What they really want is not your haircut, it's your hair!"

About five years ago, I grew restless again. There was about a year of temptation to make a change before I was ready to actually do it. And then there was the question of who would do it. Ricky had always said to me, "If you ever want to do something radical, like cut bangs, please don't ask me to do it. I hate feeling responsible for girls freaking out when they make a big change."

I came to the conclusion that if I was going to cut some serious inches off my hair, I had to be in willing hands. As I hadn't paid for

a haircut in more than a decade, I told myself that a splurge would be justified. I did my research among friends and chose a guy—let's call him "Courtney"—for my hair makeover. He cut hair in his home, not some generic salon, and I trusted the girls who recommended him.

Courtney was smart about easing me into shorter hair. He said we would start non-radically and just take a few inches off, and then, when I was ready, I was welcome to come back any time—a day, a week, a month later to go further. It took two visits over a couple of weeks to get it to the right length, but when it was finished I was over the moon. It had the appearance of being a bob, but he thinned it enough so that my thick hair didn't resemble a broom, and it was slightly shorter in the back than in the front, giving it the tiniest bit of an edge. I *loved* it. And so did everyone else—the feedback from my friends was unanimously positive.

But three months later, the cut was grown out—it had lost its shape and was hitting my shoulders, thus losing a bit of its chic. I was used to cutting my hair twice a year, max, so I therefore thought if I cut it shorter, it would last for longer.

Therein lies the mistake. The same style didn't work so well shorter, and it just wasn't the same shape as the first time. I went back twice, trying to find the bliss my first haircut resulted in. It wasn't to be found. All my subsequent visits did was make my hair even shorter, until finally my bob was up to my ears. My hair was too thick for this, no matter how much it was thinned. The long-feared dread planted itself in my chest, and I got that terrible feeling of regret. If only I could rewind life an hour back, I could stop myself from trying to fix it again and just grow it out. I just found it terribly hard to accept that the same person couldn't give me the same haircut twice. Or that if you spent enough money on a haircut, it couldn't possibly go wrong!

The wisdom in bad haircuts finally came to me from (who else?) Diane von Furstenberg. Sporting my newly shorn 'do, I walked into her office. She looked up, paused, gave me a sympathetic look, and said, "What happened, darling?" Before I could answer, she

started to giggle. It was a loving giggle, but she was laughing at me nonetheless. I just sat down, shook my head from side to side, and looked at her, feeling pathetic that I was so upset about a silly haircut. Or maybe I felt pathetic that I was finding myself in this place, yet again. Before I could respond, she said, "Don't worry. All women need a good dose of humility from time to time. Few things are as effective as a bad haircut."

That was it. I got it after that. Whether intentional or not, deserved or not, the universe delivered me bad haircuts from time to time to keep me humble. It didn't make the process any less painful, but it did help me to accept it.

How is my hair now? I've kept it at shoulder length. My long hair now seems too much like "the old me" and a bit too bohemian. Keeping it shorter is for sure more maintenance—frequent cuts, some styling required—but it suits the more classic American, Lauren Hutton–ish look I'm going for these days.

All this haircut humility became small potatoes in the summer of 2010 when I noticed a bump on my nose. *It's most likely a pimple*, I thought. I picked at it a few times to no avail. Then I squeezed it with tweezers, which only made it redder. And yet when I finally had the good sense to leave it alone, it just got bigger. And bigger. Within ten days, I had convinced myself that I had grown a wart on my nose, just like a witch! It made sense—I had been treating some warts on my son's knee, and I must have gotten some of the virus on my hands and then touched my nose. How embarrassing. What a pain! How was the doctor going to get rid of the wart on my nose without leaving—*gasp!*—a scar? I made an emergency appointment with my dermatologist. I suspected he would probably send me to someone else as he often did with any nonmedical issues I had. Dr. Prioleau is a cancer specialist, not a person who takes away unwanted bumps. Because my mom has, thanks to Dr. Prioleau, survived melanoma three times, I have been to see him every six months since I was a teenager to ensure I am not following in her path. So I walked into his office, slightly sheepish at the

notion of bothering him with something so mundane as a wart, and sat myself down on the examining table.

"Do I have a wart on my nose??" I asked in a slightly high-pitched tone.

"Let me take a look."

I think he already knew but wanted to look at the bump magnified before making any pronouncements.

"No, it's not a wart. I'm pretty sure it's a squamous cell carcinoma."

Carcinoma was the only word I heard before I started wishing I had a wart on my nose. It turns out that the kind of skin cancer I had was not as bad as melanoma, but worse than basal cell, the most common and benign form. He scraped the bump off my nose with a scalpel and said I would have to come back in a week for more extensive Mohs surgery. He would cut a bit deeper into the place where the bump had been and test the flesh to make sure there was no cancer in it. If there was, he'd go even deeper until the boundaries were all clear. If not, I'd be all set. Then he would send me four blocks uptown to see the plastic surgeon who would close the wound. I asked as many questions as I could think of and relaxed when Dr. Prioleau assured me that if I did the complete treatment, this bump on my nose wouldn't shave even a day off my life.

"Whatever it takes," was my response.

So now I had a Band-Aid on my nose—quite a noticeable one—and that following weekend we were due to attend my husband's ex-wife's wedding. Talk about humility! She and I had become friends, good friends, actually, but I couldn't help but think I was having to pay some karmic debt by going to her wedding with a bandage across the middle of my face. My embarrassment was even more heightened by the fact that the wedding was taking place at Anna Wintour's house and would be photographed for *Vogue*. But what was there to do? I put on my prettiest Thakoon floral dress, made damn sure I was having a good hair day, found the smallest round Band-Aid to cover up the hole in my nose, and went along to the wedding. Needless to say, my picture didn't make it into *Vogue* that time.

My surgery was scheduled for July 1. Coco would be off at summer camp by then, and Christopher had gone to England for a couple of weeks. It would just be Zach and me at home. It didn't occur to me that I might want my husband around for this ordeal.

I can't say whether I didn't understand the magnitude of what I was about to endure or whether I was in denial. Whatever the case, worry started to creep in as soon as Dr. Prioleau entered the operating room.

"You must be really brave," he said upon entering.

"Why?"

"Because you're very calm, and it's rare that a patient doesn't call me many times before having surgery on their face."

"Well, what choice do I have? There is cancer on my face and we need to get rid of it."

"Yes, exactly, but most patients aren't that rational. They beg and bargain for an alternative, but this is the best and safest way to make sure all the cancer is gone."

I didn't see the point in begging or bargaining, but the conversation did suggest that maybe I was in for more than I expected.

"I'm going to remove as little of your nose as I possibly can, okay?"

"Okay." Fuck.

Obviously, the most painful part of the surgery was the large syringe of local anesthetic being injected into the tip of my nose. It hurt so much that my eyes welled up, but I was able to blink away the tears.

Dr. Prioleau did his work with the scalpel, wrapped my face in gauze to keep the wound from bleeding, and then disappeared for a half hour to test the flesh for cancer. I just lay there wondering what the hell I was in for.

"All clean," he announced when he reentered the room. "The thing with these kind of cancers is that eighty percent of the time, the biopsy removes all of the cancer, but we have to cut in deeper just to be sure."

Great, so I would have been just fine with the bump removed flush from my nose, but *just to be sure* it was necessary to dig in deeper. That thought has stayed with me.

222

"So you have about a one-centimeter-diameter hole on the right side of your nose. It's about the size of your pupil."

That was the precise moment when I realized why he'd been surprised that I was so calm about this whole event. A fucking hole in my nose the size of my pupil??? God, I wished it had been a wart.

"I'm going to put in three or four stitches. See what the plastic surgeon says, but you may be able to get away with just that."

I left Dr. Prioleau's office and got into a cab.

My heart hurts even now just writing about this. I remember realizing the gravity of what was going on and how I was going to have to adjust to a new me. Back then, in that moment, I didn't know if I was ever going to look the same again. I gave myself a few minutes to mourn my nose. The thing is—and this may sound vain, but I'm sure everyone can relate to having a favorite feature— I *really* loved my nose. Kevyn Aucoin, the famous makeup artist, once told me that I had a perfect nose—the right size, shape, and proportion to my face. He even took a picture of it once, so he could show it to friends who were getting nose jobs!

I also felt very alone in that moment. I don't regret having been alone. I'm sure I would have been so much less brave if my husband had been there. And if my mother or sisters had been there, then I would have had to deal with their reactions to my face-changing, life-altering moment as well as my own. I wouldn't have blamed them—how could they not have felt my pain? But I didn't want to have to reassure them as well as myself.

I pulled myself together when I got out of the cab and went into the discreet side door to the left of a big, fancy, canopied entrance on Park Avenue. There were two other women in the waiting room. With two giant Band-Aids placed across the bridge of my nose, I'm sure they thought I was there for a nose job checkup. *Oh, who cares?* I thought.

I was called into a small examining room before we went into the main operating room. Dr. LaTrenta removed the Band-Aids, winced slightly, and told me that I was beautiful and that I would continue to be beautiful. I don't know if this made me feel better

or worse. I had gotten over myself—for just a minute—and didn't really want to think about beauty. I was trying to focus on what my mother told me and always, *always* emphasized—that health is everything in life. Despite being a stunning woman herself, my mom almost never talked about beauty with my sister or me when we were growing up. She didn't comment much on our looks or judge the way we dressed ourselves, but she always encouraged us to take good care of ourselves—to see the very best doctors and to eat and exercise in a way that made us feel good. Never had I felt more grateful for this perspective. I was a mother of two young children and the wife of a man who I adored. What did my nose matter if I had my health? If I had the ability to live a full life with the people I loved most in the world?

Still in the small room, Dr. LaTrenta told me we had a decision to make. He could either use fewer stitches, resulting in a smaller scar but in a different-shaped nose or he could use more stitches, resulting in a bigger scar, but maintaining the shape of my original nose. For option two, he would have to slice a vertical line up the bridge of my nose and then pull down the loose skin to cover the hole—it's called flap surgery and it's been proven very successful because skin can stretch quite far when pulled vertically. I went for the flap surgery—I preferred to have a bigger scar than to change the actual landscape of my face. He agreed.

On the operating table, I fell back into the feelings of fear and loneliness. Feeling safe behind the gauze covering my eyes, tears fell freely down my cheeks. I took slow, deep breaths and tried to orient myself to my new reality, not even knowing exactly what it would be. It was still entirely possible that I wouldn't ever look the same again, that I wouldn't look like me.

I left Dr. LaTrenta's office with twenty stitches in my nose and some serious painkillers. I got in a cab, called my husband, and sobbed into the phone all the way home. At no point had I seen a mirror since the whole day began. This was not a mistake. Dr. LaTrenta suggested I not look at my nose for a whole week, but I knew I wouldn't have the discipline to do that. When I walked

into the house, I made the miscalculation of taking off the Band-Aid for my little sister and my son, Zach, before I even looked at it myself. I guess I was eager to finally share with someone the anxiety and heartache of what I had been through that day. I could see the shock and sadness on their faces before they even knew what to say. Then, my sweet, lovely Zach walked over to me with such a sincere and sympathetic look, put the palm of his hand on my cheek, and said, "Don't worry, Mommy. You're still beautiful and you still look like my mommy." Not able to stop the flow of tears, I kissed him, walked into my bedroom, and shut the door. I sobbed some more. Then I went into the bathroom where the mirrors were.

The line of stitches looked like an upside-down question mark with the circular part on the tip and the long line going up the right side. My nose was unrecognizable. It was red and quite swollen. I tried to remember that Dr. LaTrenta had promised the shape of my nose would eventually return.

I rang my close friend and former life coach Regena, who was meant to be my date for the Lady Gaga concert that night. She now lived in my building, and our relationship had evolved from student and teacher into friends. If anyone could empower me in that moment, I knew she could. She came up, checked me out, and said, "Wow, sister, you've had some day. What time are we going out?"

My eyes widened at the thought. But when I looked at her, she nodded, as if to say "You better believe we're going out." So out we went an hour later, with two large Band-Aids horizontally covering my nose. I saw someone I knew at the restaurant we went to but managed to avoid eye contact. And I saw two friends at the concert, one who recognized me and expressed obvious concern and the other who didn't seem to register that it was me behind the bandages, and I didn't care to point it out. Regena and I had a fun night. Because of the painkillers I was a step removed from my new reality and the distraction of Lady Gaga's performance helped me not to focus on it too much.

The next morning was the real shocker. I got up early and went into the bathroom expecting to be used to my new look.

But both eyes were black-and-blue, and the whole right side of my face had swollen up. Worse, my nose had blown up, too, leaving behind any resemblance of its former self. The only reason I went into the office that morning was to get out of the house before Zach saw me. And since I was in the office, I thought, I might as well go ahead with a few appointments. I was at WME at the time, and I was due to meet with R. J. Cutler, the director of *The September Issue*, that morning to discuss a potential new project. I had never met R.J., but I thought I had better warn him before he came upon the sight of me, unsuspecting of the horror that lay before him. I rang him up and explained that I looked like a battered housewife, and as long as he was okay with that, I was happy to have the meeting.

"No worries," he replied. "I think I can manage that."

When R.J. walked into my office, his eyes widened at the sight of me, and then he did the sweetest thing. He walked straight over to the window and summoned me over. He pulled back the hair hanging down over his forehead and showed me a scar next to his hairline.

"I had a big line of stitches on my face, too, that I thought would change how I looked forever, but check it out—now I have to walk over to the sunlight in the window to make the scar noticeable enough for you to see. You're going to heal just fine."

I am not always a positive-thinking person, but when given the option between living in fear and deciding things just might work out okay, I am always in favor of the latter. That moment in my office with R.J. was the moment I decided I was going to carry on with my life as normal, despite the scary condition of my face. I willed myself to believe that at some point in the future I would feel like myself again.

But not without some serious self-pity first. After R.J. left, I sat down in front of my giant Mac desktop screen—the kind so big that it just about blocks your view of the rest of the room—and turned on the Photobooth app. I was going to snap some pics of myself and send them to my husband, who was still in England. I

was fine that he was away, but I still had the urge to show him what he'd missed out on. To show him how brave I'd been on my own. To show him how shocking I looked.

I unpeeled the two Band-Aids lying across the stitches on my nose *very* slowly, not because they hurt, but because I didn't want them to pull the scar apart. The tissue on my nose had swelled up now around the black stitches, and it all looked ugly and messy and angry. Not wanting to dwell too long, I snapped a few pics and sent them off with no note attached to the e-mail. I thought the images would speak for themselves.

"WOW!" was Christopher's one-word response when he wrote back a few hours later.

Next I had to decide if I was going to board the flight to Los Angeles that I was scheduled to be on that evening. Yes, I was meant to fly across the country that very day. In all my pre-op naiveté, it never occurred to me that my little nose bump would get in the way of a long-planned trip to California to attend a Chanel event I had helped plan. But more important, I had promised to take Zach, whose best friend had moved to L.A. the year before. They missed each other terribly and got to see each other only on the rare occasion. Plus, with Coco at sleepaway camp and Christopher in England, this was Zach's big treat for the summer. I desperately wanted to take him, but going meant that I would also have to go to the Chanel party looking like *this*. Chanel had paid for my ticket, and they (and my boss) would certainly understand if I canceled because I wasn't well enough to travel, but would they understand if I used their ticket and stayed in their hotel room but didn't go to the party? I didn't think so.

At eight o'clock that evening, Zach and I boarded our Virgin America flight to LAX. As we walked down the aisle to our seats, I saw people stare, or look at me and then look away quickly before I registered their discomfort, or look at me until I met their eyes so they could give me a look of sympathy. None of it felt particularly good, but I quickly distracted myself by focusing on getting myself and Zach settled into our seats. The housekeeper at the

227

house where Zach's friend lived was even less subtle. "You got a nose job?" she asked as she walked us through the house.

Four days later, it was the morning of the Chanel party. The purple lines under my eyes were fading, and the swelling around my nose was slowly retreating. Still, I was nowhere close to looking like me, and the oversize Band-Aids weren't helping my cause. I went to the local drugstore in search of the most tasteful Band-Aids I could get my hands on. Tasteful Band-Aids? I laughed at myself. What does that even mean? But in my own mind I knew exactly what I was looking for. Something that was fabric instead of plastic and big enough to cover my stitches (I would still need two to do the job), but that would not extend much beyond the sides of my nose. I was also after the color of Band-Aid that would most closely match my skin tone. I went to one of those giant drugstores that also sell granola bars and fruit punch and beach chairs in hopes that they would have the largest selection. I found a Band-Aid box that had various shapes and sizes of the fabric ones I was after and settled on those. The result was a huge improvement.

For the party, I put on a very pretty off-white crochet dress with a marine blue stripe at the bottom from Chanel. I wore killer Roger Vivier heeled sandals that brought out the blue in my dress and the blue in my eyes. I felt as pretty as I could with a mangled face. And off I went.

The Chanel party was in Malibu. Ron Meyer, the head of CAA, had agreed to host it at his beautiful oceanfront home. Chanel was a client of WME, and they had asked us to come up with a celebrity face for their new J12 Marine Bleu men's watch. We hired world-champion surfer Laird Hamilton to lend the watch a sporty, rugged, masculine feel—an image not easy to accomplish when thinking about the Chanel brand. I walked up the long driveway toward the massive, sleek, white, flat-roofed house. Near the front door was a girl with a clipboard and next to her was my longtime friend, PR guru Nadine Johnson, the one who was responsible in large part for my meeting Christopher.

"DARLING!" she said when she saw me, excited and concerned by my look at the same time. "What happened to you?"

I knew this was the first of a chorus of "What happened??"s I would hear all night from people I knew and didn't know.

I suddenly wondered whether I'd made the right decision to go. All I had considered was how I was going to feel at the party. I hadn't thought through the possibility that people's shock at my appearance would dominate the party chatter or the attendees' gazes. But eventually it wore down and everyone got over it. The sun set, the people I knew had all expressed their concern for me, and after a glass of wine (or three) I let go and forgot about it myself for a little while.

I remember the exact moment a few weeks later when I began to believe that I was, in fact, going to look like myself again one day. The stitches had been removed, but Dr. LaTrenta had not shown me a mirror before covering up the wound with medical tape and instructing me not to take it off for a week. Only then could I look at my nose and judge it, he urged. It would still be months before the swelling and redness would go away completely, but he promised that the shape of my nose would begin to resemble itself again. It was a long wait, but on the seventh day after my visit to Dr. La-Trenta, I was driving to my sister's apartment to visit her. The tape had lost its stickiness at the sides and was beginning to curl up. Before I got out of the car and went upstairs, I decided to take a peek. I slowly lifted the tape up and over the bridge of my nose. The skin had healed enough to stay together without the help of an adhesive. I still had the upside-down-question-mark-shaped line from where the stitches had been, and it was really red. But the healing had made good ground, and it looked better than I expected. My sister agreed that a month out from the operation, the result was better than she had hoped. Despite the shock and drama of the first few days, I was well on my way to drawing less attention to myself.

I wore the tape for three more weeks and then I let my nose heal naturally in the fresh air, applying silicone gel in the morning and keeping it strictly out of the sun.

It's now been five years. People have stopped asking me how I got the scar on my nose, but sometimes I catch the sight of it in the cruel fluorescent light of an elevator at an unforgiving angle and think, soberly, *Wow—there's my scar.* The redness has gone down, although it flares up with a glass of wine or a rush of cold air, and I put concealer on it when I apply makeup. But the real miracle is the shape of my nose. It is identical to the shape it has always been. I sometimes look at it in the mirror and wonder how Dr. LaTrenta managed to conceal that huge one centimeter hole on the tip of my nose without grafting skin. It's amazing. And every time I see Dr. Prioleau, he takes a good look at it to see how it's healing, and he praises me once again for being brave. I recently told him that he doesn't have to do that anymore. I'm over it.

I *am* over it. I am grateful to have recovered from my bout with skin cancer relatively unscathed, and I am grateful for the "good dose of humility" it gave me. When I want to, I can make my scar disappear completely, but I don't always want to. It's a good reminder of my own strength, independence, and confidence in myself, apart from the appearance of my face.

Applying NARS Schiap lipstick just before putting on my wedding dress, 2001.

DESPITE YEARS of having my hair and makeup professionally done for shoots, or paying someone to do it for a big night out, I've never been so happy with my beauty routine as I have been since learning to do it for myself.

When I was planning my wedding at age twenty-six, I still knew very little about makeup. For both day and evening, I wore little more than mascara (top lids only) and lip gloss (always in a neutral color), and maybe a bit of eyeliner. What I did know was that whenever I had had my makeup "done," I often felt *over*done. I just didn't recognize myself. So when faced with the

prospect of wedding makeup, I was terrified of not being happy with the result on such an important occasion. Sure, I could have tried a few different makeup artists and had a trial run in advance, but that all sounded too high maintenance for me. Instead, I found some inspiration pictures online and took them up to the Saks store on Fifth Avenue for a makeup lesson. When I got there, I made a beeline for the NARS counter (my favorite beauty brand) and explained my quest for wedding-day makeup know-how. After some trial and error and finally achieving a perfected look all on my own, I left the store armed with a bagful of makeup and new skills to match. I still look back at my wedding pictures, pleased that I was able to create the best version of myself while still looking like me.

My hair took longer to figure out on my own. As any girl knows, good hair comes and goes for everyone depending on the weather, the shampoo you use, how you brush your hair, how often you wash it, how it dries, how long it's been since you washed it, and on and on. I also found, to my great frustration, that getting my hair professionally done was no guarantee that it would look how I wanted it to, either. Even with my favorite hairdressers, I've found that over the years every blowout or curling set is different, some better than others. At one point I was seeing a girl at Frédéric named Nicole. She worked wonders on my hair with a curling iron. She just subtly amped up the volume on my own natural waves without making my hair look "done." She would have me wash my hair at home, let it air-dry to bring out the movement and texture, and then she would just put in a few extra curls—two in front, two on each side, and one in back. After a while—bless her—she told me that I could easily learn how to do the curls myself and save a whole lot of time and money in the process. She showed me how to roll the curls out and back to get them going in the right direction. She taught me to clamp the iron down an inch from the bottom of my hair and stop the curl about five inches from my part—this gives the curl a more seventies modern vibe as opposed to Grace Kelly "lady" curls. And finally she showed me how to space the curls so they left room for my natural waves to mingle among the manufactured ones. Sounds simple. It wasn't. The first time I tried this at home was not particularly successful. I probably would have given up were it not for a wedding I went to in South America weeks later where there was no one to do my hair but me. Armed with my new curling iron, I tried the curls again. Much better this time, especially with the humidity making my own waves

bigger and more defined. Years later, I am still not a master of self-styled hair, but I've figured out that no matter how good it looks just after I've done it, it always looks better the next day. So if I really care how my hair will look for a given day, I make sure to whip out my curling iron the day before.

When I was in New York, I would still hire the pros for my hair and makeup on special occasions, like for the CFDA Awards and the Met Ball— it gave me the chance to try new things (like metallic turquoise liquid eye-liner—LOVE!) and learn new skills. But now that I'm in England it's hard to imagine getting someone else to style me. I think every woman should know how to do her own hair and makeup to maximum effect. It's like having your own exercise routine, your own salad dressing recipe, or your own favorite pair of jeans—it helps you feel more confident in who you are.

My finished wedding look, with Mom in tow.

233

REJECTION IS A MANDATORY REST STOP ALONG THE ROAD TO SUCCESS

I STILL REMEMBER the first time I went to Barneys New York. It was 1986, and we were living in Bronxville. My parents were very generous about taking us into the city for important cultural events, an occasional dinner at a new restaurant, or to celebrate a holiday or a birthday. Other times we'd venture into the city on a random Saturday or Sunday just to explore a new neighborhood or have a change of scenery. Such was the basis for which we ventured down to Seventeenth Street and Seventh Avenue to check out the opening of the new Barneys New York, "the coolest store in New York," as my parents billed it. We wandered the spiral staircase up through the atriumlike space, so visually stimulated that we didn't know where to look next. My mom bought an embroidered chalet scarf that she still wears today, and my stepfather bought some socks and a tie. Even then, at twelve years old, I could appreciate why the store was so novel—it was open, airy, and light, unlike other department stores. It had *so many* things I liked but had never seen before, and the atmosphere was welcoming, approachable, happy. Walking around the floor at Barneys was satisfying in and of itself, without even having to buy anything.

Opposite: Heading to fashion shows at Lincoln Center in head-to-toe Reed Krakoff. Garance Doré took this picture of me. I love how she photographs women.

235

By the time I graduated from college, Barneys had opened an uptown outpost on Madison Avenue and Sixty-First Street. Again, it impressed. The ground floor was covered with beautifully hand-laid mosaic tiles, there were glass tanks filled with exotic fish and sea creatures everywhere, and each floor had its own unique character. By then, Barneys had launched CO-OP, the lower-priced floor for the younger customer, and slowly I had worked my way up to be able to afford just the occasional piece, or an outfit on sale. In those years I bought a checked wool blazer from Theory, two pairs of Chaiken and Capone trousers, a black silk dress and a navy brocade suit both by Philosophy di Alberta Ferretti, a pair of shocking-pink suede Ann Demeulemeester Mary Janes, a Voyage skirt complete with the signature velvet ribbon and beaded fringe hem, and a million-ply cashmere sweater from Narciso Rodriguez (on final sale, of course) that I wear to this day.

In 2010, my first interview—the unofficial one—for the job of Barneys' fashion director actually took place at a charity dinner. Anna Wintour and Diane von Furstenberg were being honored by New York and Co. for their contributions to Fashion's Night Out, a festive night of shopping on the eve of Fashion Week that was intended to revitalize the retail economy after the recession. Everyone in the industry knew that Barneys had recently had a big management shake-up starting at the top with the hiring of Mark Lee, the new CEO, and affecting nearly every layer of the company. Many of the open positions had been filled by this point except for that of the fashion director, one of the more visible roles within any department store. Each week, it seemed, *Women's Wear Daily* would report about which potential candidates had been seen entering the Barneys building or spotted having breakfast with Mark Lee in a trendy restaurant. One or two friends had discreetly whispered in my ear that my name had come up as a possibility for the position, and so when the Barneys PR office invited me to be a guest at this charity event, I had a suspicion that it might be an informal way to test the waters with me. Conscious of this, I put together a killer outfit—"winter white" men's tailored

wool trousers with a pressed crease down the front, and a matching cashmere tunic sweater belted with a silver metal Calvin Klein belt and topped with a Thakoon patchwork fur jacket. I slicked my hair back into a neat, chic bun and wore just enough makeup to look healthy and cheerful in mid-December. Before we even sat down at dinner, Daniella Vitale, Mark Lee's right-hand woman, asked me if I would be interested in interviewing for the job. "Yes!" I said, without much thought. Then I was seated next to Mark Lee and we chatted away about "the new Barneys," my favorite designers, and my thoughts about the history of the store and how to carry it forward. I was inspired.

Official interviews with Daniella and eventually with Mark followed, and I found myself feeling confident that I was qualified, perhaps even the right person, for the job. But was the job right for me? My friends were divided. A few were concerned for me. Knowing me in the context of my family, they found it hard to imagine me compromising on any part of being a wife and mother. One friend who knows me very well and has decades of experience on the fashion month circuit said to me bluntly, "That is *so not* the right job for you, Amanda." But there was a part of me that figured maybe all the investment I had made in my family had paid off, and maybe the time had come when I was able to afford greater independence and freedom in the work choices I made. The kids were in a great place at that moment, and my husband, who is always supportive, offered to pick up the slack for me like I often had done for him.

Other friends couldn't believe I was even questioning whether the job—should it be offered to me—was the best direction to take. It was one of the most coveted jobs in fashion! It was the perfect culmination of all my previous jobs! The job included all the things I loved doing! Francisco Costa, designer at Calvin Klein, grabbed me by the shoulders in my living room one Saturday morning, looked me straight in the eye, and said, "Are you kidding me?" when I expressed my reservations. "You were born to do this job!" he continued. The part that resonated with me the most was that

the duties associated with the job truly were all the things I most loved doing. I beamed when I read the job description—attending all fashion shows, presentations, and showroom appointments; helping to shape the buys; choosing the looks to be featured in the catalogues and advertising; discovering new designers; working on the design and merchandising of the Barneys private-label collections; overseeing fashion displayed on mannequins and in store windows; compiling and presenting trend presentations; and having my own regular blog on the Barneys website. It sounded so perfect, a true dream job.

There was also a third factor in my decision-making process, but perhaps it was not so far in the forefront of my consciousness at the time. I had been through a similar process a few years earlier with *Vanity Fair*, interviewing for the same position—fashion director—of the magazine. I was unsure when I was asked to interview because I had recently left Tuleh and had devoted myself to forging my own way in the industry after working for so many "name brands" and was deep in the trenches of writing *I Love Your Style*. But, the job description and the allure of that title had captured my imagination. After my initial interview with the managing editor, I was invited to come back and meet with Graydon Carter, the editor in chief.

I had prepared for meeting Graydon very much in the same way as I had for meeting Mark Lee, by ensuring that my clothes would make a strong first impression. I didn't have much income of my own at the time and my closet was filled entirely with Tuleh (the brand I had just broken up with), so I decided to wear vintage. I had a sixties black wool dress with brown mink collar and cuffs. It was "just fashion enough" to look relevant but not over the top. I then mixed my best bracelet—a walnut-and-gold chain-link one from Seaman Schepps—with some funky seventies ones I'd found at a thrift shop in London. I carried my brown YSL ostrich Muse bag (a gift from the designer) and wore black opaque tights and black suede stiletto boots from Manolo Blahnik, which I'd bought years earlier.

"Aren't you cold?" was the first thing Graydon asked me, referring to the unseasonably cold early-winter day, when I walked in his office. Before I could answer, he continued, "Well, I suppose you have a car waiting for you downstairs."

"I took the subway," I responded dryly. I am a subway girl. Always have been. Especially during Fashion Week. When the tents were at Bryant Park, I could get on the F train a block from my house and get off right at the park entrance. Riding the subway, especially when overdressed, is a quintessential part of the New York experience. Even years later when I was fashion director at Barneys and wearing Alaïa heels to work every day, I slid on my Repettos morning and evening to walk down the stairs to the train.

I could tell he was impressed that I took the subway, but he was right about me being freezing cold. There was a problem with the dress I was wearing—because of the fur on the cuffs I couldn't fit a coat over it. It wouldn't be the first or the last time I suffered for fashion.

Anyway, Graydon and I talked for an hour and a half and I felt that it couldn't have gone better. He told me all about the nice things that friends and former employers in the industry had said about me. And we discussed the fact that while I was an unusual candidate for the job, having not actually worked at a magazine before, I certainly had a lot of experience within the industry, and perhaps my outsider view would bring a fresh perspective.

The next day, Graydon's managing editor called to say how much Graydon liked me and that they were going to start calling my references. I was now completely swept up in the fantasy of having this job and feeling hopeful that it just might be offered to me. But then a few days passed, and then a couple of weeks passed, and I didn't hear anything from *Vanity Fair*. I would eventually get a lovely note from Graydon telling me that I didn't get the job. I never did get an explanation for why the job was given to someone else—was it my lack of magazine experience? Did office politics get in the way? I'll never know. Regardless, I was gutted. I had never been rejected professionally like that before, and it stung.

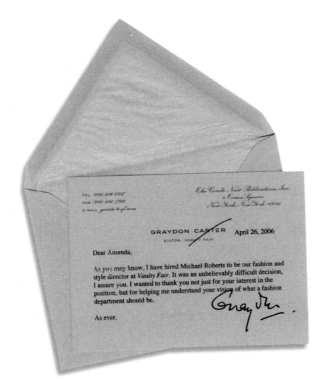

The gracious rejection letter I received from Graydon Carter. It has motivated me ever since.

Of course I can see now that it was good for me to have had that experience of great expectation and the ensuing disappointment, but I can also see that when the second chance came around to be a fashion director, my ambition to succeed this time may have colored my decision-making process, whether I was fully aware of it or not.

Despite the equally compelling arguments from both sides regarding the Barneys job, what proved irresistible was this idea that the job would give me access to all the designers I knew and wanted to know. I would encourage them in growing their brands wisely and effectively. I would support them and challenge them. To be the fashion director of Barneys truly would be my arrival at that place on the horizon—as a champion for designers—that I had plotted out with Mark Flashen years earlier. And, just a few days after I made up my mind, the job was mine.

point of view. I don't know about you, but when I go out for a day in the city, I am usually carrying the biggest bag I can possibly manage and am headed for the subway. The first problem is the bag—it's not possible to sling a bag over your shoulder when your coat is delicately resting there. Second, navigating crowded stairs with people rushing and squeezing past you is pretty much a guarantee that your coat will be pushed off your shoulders and onto the ground.

I've come to the conclusion that the "coat over my shoulders" look is only allowed in the evening, when I am delicately navigating my way into a cab and am carrying only a clutch in my hands. Plus, I love the contrast of a tailored jacket or coat thrown over a far more feminine and delicate dress or blouse. It's that "I'm cold so my boyfriend gave me his jacket" look.

If you find a look that doesn't work for your general lifestyle, find a time or place that it would better suit and look forward to those moments.

Fashion editor Virginie Mouzat gracefully pulling off the coat over her shoulders look—in leopard no less!

Hannah Henderson (left) and Meredith Melling (opposite) are both equally successful mixing denim in their own way.

DO YOU mix denim? I do. It took me a while to get my head around how it works, but I eventually figured out how I like it. Right now mixing denim is a trend, but it's also a classic concept that never goes out of style, so I just carry on whether it's in or out of fashion. What works for me is a denim or chambray shirt (unbuttoned as far as you dare to go) worn with jeans—either skinny or flared. Think seventies Farrah Fawcett without the winged-out hair. But here's the thing—there's a delicate balance between color and texture. I like to create a balance between the two. If my shirt was on the pale side of denim and new, then I would choose jeans that were also pale but more worn looking, even with holes in them. So the colors match, but the textures are contrasting. On the other hand, you could contrast the colors—pale denim on top, dark denim on the bottom. But then I would wear a thinner chambray shirt with darker raw denim jeans, again, creating some contrast. Putting together denim is easier than it sounds; it's just a matter of trial and error until you like what you see.

UPDATED CLASSIC

OVER THE past few years, I have been most interested in following the style of girls who are bringing something new to the concept of classic style. It's not that anything is getting reinvented, but girls such as Vanessa Traina, Gaia Repossi, and Emmanuelle Alt are wearing timeless pieces such as chunky-knit sweaters, loafers, jeans, blazers, pumps, and button-down shirts in a newly simple and refined way. You could call it minimalist classic, but to me that conjures up ideas of conceptual clothes that have nothing to do with what I am talking about. Of course these clothes are new and made of more modern materials that perhaps lend a sharper, chicer look to them, but on the whole they are pieces that could have existed in most any of the past five decades, worn with a new eye toward interesting proportion and a sense of discipline to just wear a great shirt, a great pair of trousers, and a great pair of shoes, without adding all sorts of bells and whistles. Sounds easy? Not so much. Although I aspire to this style, I often find myself adding a scarf, or a bracelet, or buying a print I fall in love with that ruins the simplicity of the look. Live and learn, I guess. And in the meantime, I'll put these girls up on a pedestal!

Opposite: Vanessa Traina reinvents the jeans and a sweater look.

245

OF ALL THE PLACES IN THE WORLD TO FALL APART, I NEVER THOUGHT IT WOULD HAPPEN IN PARIS

WHEN I accepted the job as fashion director of Barneys, I couldn't help but think of that long-held ambition to sit in the front row of the Paris shows, dating back to when I worked for Patrick all those years before. Finally, I would go to every show I had dreamed about—Céline! Balenciaga! Balmain! Rick Owens! Isabel Marant! I would then go to all the showrooms to see and touch the clothes up close. I would slowly flip through the racks, considering each item one at a time. I would decide which outfits I thought were best for the advertising, the catalogues, the windows. I would help the buyers decide which were the most important looks to order, and I would plot carefully and choose my best angle of argument if they disagreed. Maybe I would even get to try on a piece or two. My first day at Barneys took place two days before the start of fashion month, as we call it in the industry. New York Fashion Week was up first. My assistant gave me my schedule, which plotted out nine days of back-to-back shows, buying appointments, and fashion parties followed by a weekend off. I'd have the following Monday in the office, and then on Tuesday I would leave for five days in Milan, followed by ten days in Paris. My travel schedule started

Opposite: In Paris for the shows, wearing an Olatz silk shirt, Rag & Bone pants, and Céline sunglasses.

at eight A.M. and finished around ten P.M., not including dinner. No days off.

The hours were fine. I'd done it before and could do it again. Sure, the idea of keeping that pace for a whole month was intimidating, but I was so excited to get going, to see all the fashion, and to have a say. I was inspired by the feeling that I was playing an important, coveted role in the industry that I loved and had been a part of for so long.

Truth be told, I have never been a big fan of Milan—I had spent a lot of lonely weeks working there in the past, and I never quite got over the feeling of gloom that descended upon me whenever I arrived. But Paris . . . Paris would be my treat at the end of the long weeks ahead of me.

When I arrived in Paris at the end of that first fashion month, I was pretty cross-eyed. But nonetheless, I was so happy to be there. I arrived on a Monday evening, and I would have a few coveted hours off on Tuesday morning before seeing Anthony Vaccarello's show that afternoon. I slept in for the first time in three weeks, I washed my hair, and then I set out to explore the area surrounding my hotel in the sixth arrondissement. There was a Mariage Frères tea shop, my mother's favorite, where I stocked up on gifts to bring home. There was also a little Japanese shiatsu massage parlor that would become my occasional late-night stop after shows, if I could catch them before they closed. I then set out walking across Île Saint-Louis toward the Marais. I wound through the streets and arrived at rue de Saintonge, stopping at the Isabel Marant shop (for me) and Finger in the Nose (for my kids). Finally I arrived at Merci, the bohemian home-and-fashion concept store that is always my favorite stop in Paris. I lost myself browsing through the vintage furniture and kitchen supply departments, bought some linen dinner napkins, and then settled down for my all-time favorite lunch in their ground-floor café. They had this incredible buffet of healthy but satisfying vegetable salads and cold-pressed juices. After days of endless pasta eating in Italy, it was a relief to have something clean and fresh before moving on to the even

heavier French meals. When I was finished I treated myself to a giant portion of peach and raspberry crumble and a great cup of coffee and then made my way back to my hotel to start the final stretch of fashion month.

The Paris fashion show schedule was especially grueling. It was the longest, stretching out over ten days, and the most jam-packed. It was also the most crowded. On the whole, the show venues in Paris were smaller than in New York and Milan and the street-style photographers lurking outside were more abundant and aggressive. God forbid you were walking anywhere in the vicinity of Anna Dello Russo, you might get pushed out of the way or even onto the ground if you were in the way of a blogger's lens. I also had to figure out how to handle having my own picture taken. There was nowhere near the urgency to get a snap of me as there was for a veritable street-style star like Giovanna Battaglia, Taylor Tomasi Hill, or Miroslava Duma, but still I would reliably be asked by the crowd of photographers to pose for a picture. When I went to shows under my own steam, this was no problem as my time was my own. But now that I was walking in with my bosses and colleagues at Barneys, it felt wrong to linger while getting my picture taken. I learned how to just pause briefly, let them snap a pic or two, say thank you, and then keep moving. At the time, street-style photography and blogs had already made a big impact on the industry. For the fashion industry insiders—editors, buyers, writers—it was a nuisance to have the already back-to-back show schedule get jammed up by the crowds and mayhem outside. It also changed the way people dressed. Suddenly, it seemed, everyone was wearing increasingly ridiculous outfits—Color blocking! Fur! Trendy shoes! Personalized bags! Oversize jewelry!—in order to catch the eye of the bloggers. I think we all fell prey to it in one way or another, but the theatricality wore out its welcome quickly. You couldn't possibly buy enough clothes to wear a new and exciting outfit every day (at least without going broke!), and the option of borrowing clothes from designers came with its own level of exhaustion (deliveries, returns, fittings, etc.). By the time I was in Paris that first time with

Barneys, I had already pared down my wardrobe to more classic and wearable pieces. I felt good about not dressing for the photographers, and their lack of interest in my less-noticeable outfits made my show entrances and exits more manageable.

I felt the best in Paris on the days when I forced myself to get up before dawn and take a walk by the Seine, even just for twenty minutes, to calm my mind with the view and sound of water before heading out to back-to-back shows and appointments for the remainder of the day and into the night. Our day usually started with an eight A.M. coffee or breakfast meeting before the scheduled nine A.M. show. Then we raced around Paris in a car, going from show to show to show. Later in the week as the show pace slowed, we'd go to showroom appointments in between shows, to see a collection in person, have a business meeting with brand executives, and then take a look at the orders the buyers were placing. In ten days, we sat down for lunch probably two or three times. Usually, we grabbed a sandwich to eat in the car (my favorite was *saucisson sec* with butter and cornichon on a baguette) or we snacked on food served in a showroom while placing our buys. The Belgians—Ann Demeulemeester, Haider Ackermann—always had the best showroom lunch, serving homemade soups and bread, grain and vegetable salads, a board of beautiful charcuterie, and excellent coffee. Then back to shows and showrooms until we sometimes grabbed dinner, or not, before the nine P.M. show, which really started at nine thirty P.M., and got me back to my hotel by ten fifteen P.M. Maybe I have a fragile constitution, but I never understand how people socialize during the final weeks of fashion month, especially the retailers who see nearly every show and visit every showroom. I would collapse into my bed the minute I had the chance, eat a late room-service supper, catch up on work, squeeze in a Skype with the kids, and then pass out as soon as my head hit the pillow.

To say that I was overstimulated would be a huge understatement. It wasn't that I didn't thoroughly enjoy looking at fashion all day, every day throughout the previous three weeks. Or that I

Opposite: Sometimes I enjoy putting together outfits from old favorites in my closet like this Proenza Schouler skirt and Ralph Lauren camisole. I'm wearing them with a Phillip Lim belt and boots and a Céline bag and sunglasses.

wasn't inspired by the challenge and responsibility of my new role. Or that I wasn't able to handle writing trend reports, blogging, and answering urgent e-mails for two hours after I got back to my hotel so late each night. Or that talking to colleagues, peers, and coworkers all day like I was at a perpetual cocktail party hadn't worn me out. I was managing all that. The issue was that I didn't have ample time to process any of it. My brain was inundated from the minute I woke up until the minute I went to bed and then I'd do it again the next day and the next day and the next day. After a while I just started going numb. Even as I write about it, it takes me a minute or two just to remember which Céline show I first went to. The fact that sitting in the front row of my first Céline show in Paris is not forever indelibly marked in the forefront of my memory tells me that I must have been out of my mind.

This mindlessness runs counter to the very best thing about fashion. Many people love fashion for the clothes—God knows I do—but what keeps me wanting to follow it season after season, even if I didn't buy one thing for myself, is to witness and digest the progression of ideas. Following fashion is like being on a train—everyone has a similar view out of the window. For the most part, we all get tired of looking at the same thing after a while and we want to see what's next. Some people may prefer the view on the left side or the right side, or from the front of the train or out the back. Some may want to sit facing in the direction the train is moving, while others don't mind the feeling of moving backward. Some may be moved by watching the landscape, while others get more from looking at the buildings, the cars, or the people in their view. But still, we are all having similar experiences, and we all have pretty much the same references. In order to internalize all this stimulation and formulate your own point of view, reflection is essential. My experience of fashion month was like being on that train going 1,000 miles an hour—so fast that everything I saw was a blur, and it made me dizzy. It's amazing to me that I was able to make all the decisions that I did—what shows I liked, what looks I preferred, what we should advertise, what I wanted to write about, what the

most important trends were. All of those choices were made in an instant, often before the end of a four-minute runway show—all while taking photos, writing notes, and making comments to my bosses and the buyers at the same time. Some were good decisions, some not. Shows I thought I hated I ended up loving weeks later, once my brain had had the chance to digest the idea presented. Other times I declared passionate love for a look or a collection only to go off it days or weeks later, like a catchy pop song. All jammed together like this, none of it felt meaningful to me.

At the end of that first fashion week in Paris, I admitted my compromised state to myself and to my husband. I had called him the night before I came home.

"I can never do this again," I told him in all seriousness.

"Just take it one step at a time," he counseled. "You'll catch up with yourself and get some rest and it won't seem so bad in a few weeks."

But there I was again, six months later, trying to pull off that childbirth trick of forgetting the pain until you do it all over again. Little did I know this trip would be even less successful. Now I knew exactly what the month ahead would be like. From a fashion perspective, I was always very excited for the month of shows to start. As a disciple of fashion's winds of change, I was always craving new information, new inspiration, and new people added to the mix. I never knew exactly where the brilliance was going to come from, but I knew it would come from somewhere.

From a personal perspective, however, I knew fashion month would very likely bring me to my knees. The autumn round of New York Fashion Week would start the same week as the kids' new school year. Curriculum nights and parents cocktails were not in the cards for me. The worst part was being home in the same city with them but not being available to them. My husband would take over my breakfast duties for that week while I got dressed or wrote up a trend report, and then I'd get home after they'd gone to bed. It was hard on all of us to be in the same house but not really be interacting with one another. Christopher would be up when I got home, but I usually had some work to finish up or I would just

be too spent to hold a conversation. My MO was to order a thin-crust pizza from Lil' Frankie's (half mushroom, half pepperoni) and eat it in bed while watching *Oprah*.

Next was Milan. The best part of Milan was the feeling that I had to take care of only myself. I was away from the distraction/temptation of my family, and I kept in place my strict no-socializing policy to save energy for the weeks ahead. In the morning or late evening I made time to walk on the treadmill while watching endless *Modern Family* episodes in the basement gym of my hotel. I also made a commitment to myself not to drink alcohol during fashion month. Now I am a girl who *loves* my glass of wine in the evening, and this was not easy. But I didn't feel I had any room for error, energy-wise. Waking up with the slightest headache or sluggishness in the morning might just zap me of the fragile resolve I had to get myself through the month. For these reasons, Milan was always lonely. But it was short. And I knew well enough to save my energy for the final nonstop ten days ahead.

Arriving in Paris was always enormously comforting. Contrary to Milan, Paris just makes me feel happy regardless of my circumstances. Also, the fashion is always best in Paris. Sometimes it was even transformative. I remember the Haider Ackermann show that second season I was at Barneys. I had been blown away by the first show I saw, the way the girls moved down the runway to Leonard Cohen's "A Thousand Kisses Deep," the way the clothes were layered and draped over their frames, the incredibly deep and vivid jewel-tone colors. But it was so new looking and unexpected that it took me a few weeks to process it through my thoughts and my emotions. So in the next show, I was more open to what I was about to see and didn't have to think so hard about it. In the middle of one of those crazy days when you are in back-to-back-to-back shows, racing around through the Paris streets to get from one place to another in record time, that show stopped me dead in my tracks. Time stood still for just a few moments, and I was present. Fashion shows are always run at a breakneck speed—the music pulses, the girls march, I manically take notes and try to capture an in-focus photo

Opposite: Wearing a Phillip Lim fringe dress and Alaïa shoes at the Barneys party celebrating our collaboration with Carine Roitfeld.

as they whizz by me. In contrast, the Haider show that season was *slow*. But not in a torturous way (don't worry, there were those, too). In fact, I never wanted it to end. It may have been the only peaceful moment I had in Paris that season. I had the chance to tell Haider himself a few weeks later that his show may have been the only time I felt truly present during that entire fashion month. He loved it, of course, and explained that that had been his intention.

And then everything came to a roaring halt. Despite the pleasure of the beautiful city and the transformative shows, my fragile mental and emotional state suddenly decided to manifest itself physically. I was in the Christian Louboutin showroom trying on every shoe I could squeeze my not-quite-sample-size foot into, when I realized I was late for my Lanvin appointment. As I stepped off the sidewalk in my heels toward the taxi, I misjudged the height of the curb and landed awkwardly. It didn't hurt—I just noticed that it jarred me a bit. I then arrived at Lanvin, and it was decided with Scott, our salesperson, that we'd chat over lunch and then walk through the collection. A waiter brought me a plate and I sat down and inhaled it—I was always ravenous in Europe from the long hours on my feet running around. But when I got up out of my chair, I couldn't stand up straight. My back was hunched over. I sat down for a sec and then tried again. It wasn't as painful as it was just not physically possible. My lower back had locked into a curved position and wasn't budging. Thinking that movement would loosen it up, I grabbed my camera and walked around the showroom taking pictures of the shoes and bags I liked. Scott came over and asked me if I was okay. "Well, not really," I replied. "My back is stuck like this, but I am trying to move around to see if it will fix itself." He held up the satin evening clutches and jeweled sandals for me to snap so I could be done quickly and get out of there.

By the time I left Lanvin, the muscles in my lower back had begun to spasm from being held in such an unnatural position. It started to hurt. I walked down the street and got in my taxi. You'd have thought I would have gone straight back to my hotel room to lay down and call the doctor—it *was* that bad. But I was deter-

mined. My next appointment was the Céline showroom, and that was my most looked-forward-to hour of the entire fashion month. It was what made the previous three weeks bearable, knowing that Céline would be waiting there for me to bring back my enthusiasm and wonder. I did love the Céline runway shows, conceptually, but it was the commercial collection, viewable only in the showroom, that really got my blood up.

I'm sure I embarrassed myself walking into the Céline show-room like a reincarnation of the hunchback of Notre Dame. I was met by my bosses' quizzical gazes, as if to say, "What the hell happened to you?" They weren't the only ones staring. I could barely even stand up at this point. All the muscles in my entire back had seized up, and the only comfortable position was for me to squat down resting my butt on my—yes, they were Céline—high heels. I was in the middle of the showroom, crouching between the models, snapping pics manically. Time was getting shorter and shorter. It was as if my body was on a countdown. I knew that in a few minutes I wouldn't be able to move or walk at all. When I explained to my colleagues that I wasn't going to be able to go to the Paco Rabanne show that followed, they all looked relieved for me.

Back at my hotel, I rolled out of the cab and managed to make my way over to the front desk. The concierge had to come around to my side of the counter because my body was now forcibly positioned at a 45-degree angle, and I couldn't raise my head enough to look over it. When I explained what had happened, he helped me to my room, removed my shoes, and raised my legs up on the bed so I could lie on my side in the same hunched position. The hotel doctor arrived miraculously fast, but I was skeptical already. I'd been dealing with bulging discs in my back for a couple of years, and I knew exactly what had happened: One of the discs had now herniated entirely. I also knew that painkillers weren't going to be very effective, if at all. I had tried all the drugs for spinal pain available on the American market, and none had given me much relief. But he was able to give me a muscle relaxer strong enough to enable me to get around the corner to the shiatsu massage parlor. The therapist didn't speak

257

English, but I could just feel tremendous empathy in his hands. In this current state, I couldn't lay flat, so he piled up a mountain of pillows to maintain the curve of my back and to allow me to try to relax at the same time. He worked so hard to give me some relief, but when the massage was over, it hadn't done the magic I was hoping for.

I started to get panicky. I rang Diane von Furstenberg, the only person in Paris who I knew well enough to ask for help. She had lived there on occasion throughout her life, and I hoped she would know of a miracle doctor who could come rescue me.

"Get on the first plane home," she advised, saying that she didn't know where to send me in Paris, and besides, American doctors would be better for this kind of problem. I was so grateful to have a definitive answer from someone I trusted. The only trouble was, how on earth was I going to get myself home in this state? It was already ten o'clock at night. I rang the airlines and booked myself on the first morning flight at seven A.M.

It took a village to get me into a taxi that following morning at four A.M. The maid from the hotel had packed my bags for me the night before. The bellboy carried everything including my purse down to the car. The man at reception came up and escorted me down to the lobby. The taxi driver tilted the front seat all the way back so I could crawl in the car and lay on my side.

I must have looked ridiculous going through the airport. Thank God for those mini trolleys Charles de Gaulle has that allow you to push your carry-on luggage to the gate—the push bar gave me something to lean on, or rather, hunch over. As I was approaching the gate, horror struck as I realized that as it was nearing the end of Paris Fashion Week, there were bound to be people I knew on my plane. I was already woozy from all the ineffective painkillers I was on, and I was in a seriously compromising physical condition. I couldn't bear to talk to anyone.

At the gate, I couldn't sit comfortably in a chair, so I crouched down again, as I had in the Céline showroom, and rested my butt on my heels. I tried not to look around me too much for fear of making eye contact with someone I knew. But I did look up once,

Opposite, clockwise from top left: with Lazaro Hernandez of Proenza Schouler; with Alexa Chung and Carven's Guillaume Henry; with Joseph Altuzarra; with Francois Nars; with Phillip Lim; with The Row designers Mary-Kate and Ashley Olsen.

and I saw Bill Cunningham, the *New York Times* photographer, finding a seat nearby. Bill, while being a legend in the industry for many decades, is also one of the most gentle and kind men I have ever met. In that moment, he was actually a comforting sight.

I was booked in business class, and before confirming the flight I had checked to be sure that this plane had the seats that went completely flat. The only way I could tolerate the pain of lying down was to be curled up on my side. Otherwise there was no way I would have survived the eight-hour journey home.

Once on the plane, I explained to the stewardess that I wouldn't be able to sit upright in my chair for takeoff. She was unsympathetic. She told me that if I couldn't follow safety protocol I wouldn't be able to fly on the plane. My eyes pathetically welled up. There was no way I was getting off the plane, having come this far. So I lay sideways on the flat bed until we taxied down the runway, planning to put my chair up for only the briefest time. But in preparation to do so I took the whopper muscle relaxer/sleeping pill that the doctor had given me for the flight, and I don't remember anything else until we were preparing to land.

The residual effects of the medicine helped me disembark the plane and make it through immigration, despite being in a heavy mental fog. A skycap collected my bags, and I pushed an empty luggage cart to support my back while shuffling through the airport. As I came through the barrier between customs and arrivals, Christopher was standing there talking to Bill Cunningham. I overheard their conversation as I approached. "Rumor has it you shoot digital now," Christopher was inquiring of Bill.

"No, no, still shooting film," Bill insisted.

And then my husband caught sight of me, and his expression softened. His eyes were so sympathetic, and at the same time he was laughing at my ridiculous posture. It was the first time I laughed, too. It *was* funny.

Fashion girl crippled while stepping off the curb from Louboutin showroom. Further damage done at Lanvin showroom. Final nail in coffin at Céline.

We went home and I took to my bed. I would go into the hospital first thing the next morning for an epidural steroid injection that promised to have me back on my feet in three days, as if nothing ever happened, until four months later when the steroid might reabsorb back into my body and I would have to do it again. I hadn't told the kids I was coming home early. They weren't expecting me for another two days, and I thought it would be fun to surprise them. I always knew when the kids were about to arrive home from school because my dog, Ginger, would hear them in the elevator long before I could, and she would stand up and get her tail going. My nanny was in on the surprise, and when the kids came into the apartment, she asked them to go get something in my bedroom. And there I was.

The kids were so relieved to see me, and I, them. The first week I was away, I had Skyped them every day at midnight my time, six P.M. their time. They'd put the laptop on the dining table so I could "have dinner with them." It was lovely. But then my jet lag subsided, and if I was back at the hotel and finished with work before midnight, I was desperate to go to bed. At a certain point, Zach flat-out refused to talk to me. He said it was too painful to hear my voice and not have me home. Other fashion-front-row moms recounted similar stories, often on the edge of tears. Once I was sitting next to Chicago boutique owner Ikram Goldman, who is famous for having styled Michelle Obama for the inauguration and during her first few years in the White House. She asked to see pictures of my kids. When I pulled them up on my iPad and recounted to her that sweet Zach had stopped speaking to me, she burst into tears.

"Why are *you* crying?" I asked. Ikram always did fashion month with her husband and twin boys in tow.

"I just can't imagine giving up that much for fashion," she exclaimed.

I have thought about that moment with Ikram many times since. And in one sense, I felt very defeated. Fashion month, especially that last week in Paris, had long been a goal, a dream. I felt I

had utterly failed at it. I asked myself, how would it be possible for me to do this successfully? If I could redesign this scenario on my own terms, how could I make it work for me?

It had taken only about three months at Barneys to admit to myself (secretly) that I wasn't happy. I don't think I was prepared to say it out loud at that point, but in my heart I just knew it. Yes, a part of it was the shock of how much each fashion month would cost me, both physically and emotionally, but the other part was that I just couldn't find a groove in my new role. I missed the autonomy and flexibility of working independently, and it was very hard for me to find creative energy in the corporate environment of a midtown office building. I worked so hard to make myself fall in love with my new office. I spent my own money on walnut bookshelves, a vintage Moroccan rug, and a pretty desk. I installed my usual inspiration board and carted in my vintage fashion book collection. Regardless, I would often just sit at my desk and wonder how the hell I'd ended up there. Nothing felt right, and eventually I lost my confidence. I look back now and can see that many of the projects I started or worked on in my time there turned out successfully, but my insecurity in my surroundings and in the compromises I'd made to be there made me question everything I did.

I looked at Ikram, and I saw possibility. If I were to ever go to a month of fashion shows again in the future, I would have to be my own boss, and I would have to include my family in some way. Not that I would tow them all along with me—my husband would never agree to that, anyway. But I would go for less time, maybe fly home in between the weeks of shows, something like that. And it wasn't just about taking better care of my family. I would have to take better care of myself.

The third fashion week I spent in Paris during my time at Barneys wasn't much more successful, on a personal level, than the first or the second. I had already made my decision to resign from Barneys, so I knew it was to be the final marathon. I had had a second steroid injection in my spine to ensure that my back wouldn't fail me again. There was a sense of lightness about me, knowing I had

chosen my family, my sanity, and my health over this job. When my kids would call asking when I was coming home, I could reassure them that this was to be the last time. But it was a whammy of a trip. I had already flown to Rome and Milan to do the pre-fall buys in January. I was meant to go on from there to Florence to work on Barneys' private label but was thwarted by a blizzard. So I would now have to add Florence—a third leg—onto my Milan and Paris fashion month trip.

I was also planning to hand in my resignation at the end of my five days in Milan. This notion gave me a lot of anxiety. There was a knot in my stomach for weeks. It was painful to face the reality that this "dream job" wasn't for me. I could see clearly how everything I had done in my career over the past eighteen years had led me to the point, and it appeared I wasn't up for it. Had I peaked too late? Too early? After working for myself, as my own boss, for a number of years, was it too hard to go back to reporting to someone else? Was I just not a corporate girl? Was I over fashion? I considered all of these questions, but at the time I didn't have any answers. I just knew what I had to do.

Resigning went fine. Moving to England (I'll get to that in the next chapter) was a great explanation—for my bosses, for my colleagues, for the fashion press. It stopped everyone from looking for more meaningful answers. But when I arrived in Paris, I was in the elevator with my boss, and after looking in the mirror, I said to her, "God, I look really tired."

"Actually," she replied with concern, "you look drawn."

I never weigh myself, having struggled, albeit briefly, with an eating disorder in college. Wanting to lose just a few pounds, I went on the Atkins diet. After a few false starts, I got the hang of it and became perhaps *too* good at it. Having reached my goal weight, I thought, *That was easy*, and kept going for a few more. I also took on more and more exercise. In short time, I weighed 106 pounds, which on a 5 foot 9 inch frame is not funny. It would take me a year of therapy and a nutritionist to understand that "too much discipline is actually a lack of discipline," as my shrink told me.

It took me a minute to understand what my boss was alluding to, but when I looked in the mirror back in my bedroom, my face did look thin. I walked into the bathroom and stepped on the scale. I am normally 122 pounds. Over the past fifteen years, my weight has never fluctuated more than a couple of pounds more or less than that (other than during my two pregnancies).

Now, on the scale in Paris, it took me a minute to translate the kilograms to pounds in my head. The number didn't seem right, so I got out my iPhone and used the calculator. Over and over, it told me my weight was 110 pounds. Shit. How did that happen?

I thought back over the past few months. If anything, I'd been eating less healthily than I normally do because I'd been traveling so much, and in Europe no less. Pasta and panini in Italy, baguettes and foie gras in France. I couldn't figure out how it was possible that I could have lost so much weight without knowing it, without trying. I would go to my doctor for a full checkup when I got home and get a clean bill of health. No thyroid issue, no cancer eating up my insides, as I had feared in my most paranoid moments. In the end, I put my weight loss down to sheer adrenaline.

The final week in Paris was not too bad. My bosses knew I was leaving, but no one else did, apart from my husband. I enjoyed my duties more—the shows, the showrooms, the meetings—knowing that I had taken control of my life and had made an empowered, exciting decision about starting over. As scary as it was, I just knew—in my mind, body, and heart—that I was doing the right thing. The job was amazing in so many regards, but it cost me too much, as evidenced by the despair of my children and the despair of my body. Had it been ten years earlier or ten years later, it might have been the perfect place for me. But it wasn't at that moment. And I had to accept that. It was hard to do, but when I did, I was free.

The Edge Bag, my latest Céline purchase.

STYLE INFLUENCE
CÉLINE

WHEN I was writing *I Love Your Style*, I knew I had to include minimalism as one of the defining styles of our time. This was a real challenge for me—my associations with minimalism were focused on conceptual minimalism: nineties Helmut Lang, Issey Miyake, Jil Sander— an aesthetic that I didn't personally relate to and that no longer seemed entirely relevant. I did a lot of research on minimalist art, music, film, and fashion to better understand the concept and the ideas behind it. What I realized was that minimalism was really just about

265

simplicity and discipline, and that those principles could be applied to nearly any style of dressing.

Inspired by this new perspective, I started to dress in a more refined way—less jewelry, fewer layers, better quality, and more thoughtful design. It was right at this moment that Phoebe Philo started designing Céline, and that very first collection expressed, in a far more articulate way, the idea of less conceptual clothes worn in a very pared-down, timeless way. I have been a devoted disciple of Céline ever since. I can't afford that much of it, but the few pieces I do have are already among the greatest hits in my closet. Her collections have become increasingly conceptual; frankly, I just ignore that part and wait to see the more wearable and everyday items that hit the store shelves. Don't get me wrong—I am always inspired by her vision and by the risks she takes in pushing fashion forward, but as it relates to my life, she is the high priestess of great-quality, beautifully designed, wearable basics.

Opposite: Wearing a Céline runway look for a Harper's Bazaar *photo shoot, 2013.*

WHAT WAS I THINKING?

RECENTLY I have developed a little ritual that I follow when shopping for new clothes or getting dressed. I ask myself—how would I look if I wore this in one year? Five years? Ten years? It's not always easy to come up with an answer, and even when I do, it's not always right. Still, my little rule helps me rein myself in and favor more chic, classic looks over trendy ones.

If I look back at pictures of myself in my twenties and early thirties, I can't help but ask myself, sometimes even out loud, "How could you have thought that looked good?" I'm sure many women, even stylish women, have similar feelings about their sartorial past. In fact, fashion icon Chloë Sevigny once said,

"In any given month, I look back at what I was wearing the previous month and ask myself, 'What was I thinking?'" But then there are girls like Sofia Coppola, who has looked damn good consistently since her teens. Both girls have different styles, but they are both equally stylish. Sofia's look, though, is more timeless, and that is what I am going for these days.

Of course, I don't regret my ghosts of fashion moments past, as it has been those trial-and-error occasions that helped me learn my own style in the first place. But now that I have a stronger and more disciplined sense of fashion self, I'd rather invest and wear what I know will work in the long term.

SOMETIMES YOU
JUST HAVE TO
START FROM SCRATCH

THE REALIZATION that I would not last at Barneys as long as I'd hoped to came in waves, complete with high and low tides. But there were two moments, two catalysts that helped me see what my future would be if I decided to leave. The first was a lecture that Siddhartha Mukherjee gave at our kids' school about his Pulitzer-winning book *The Emperor of All Maladies: A Biography of Cancer*. When addressing why he wrote the book, he started by referring to a review of Henry Miller's book *Tropic of Cancer* by George Orwell, in which Orwell accused Miller of "living inside the belly of the whale," using the classic Bible story of Jonah and the whale as a metaphor for having a sheltered, narrow existence. Siddhartha related to this as he spent most of his time as a cancer researcher inside a small, dark laboratory in the bowels of a hospital. In writing his book, he wanted to bring the conversation of cancer "outside the belly of the whale," i.e., into the public domain. I was intrigued by this comparison, but I related to it in the opposite way. I felt that my twenty years in fashion had been spent so publicly, surrounded by people and opinions and collaborators, and I realized what I craved at that moment was some time for quiet reflection

Opposite: This picture makes me happy. I'm with my dog, Ginger, in my favorite Proenza Schouler dress, and I'm in front of the building where I live in NYC. The whole thing reminds me of the freedom and the renewed happiness I felt when I decided to leave my job.

271

and introspection. I felt the desire to retreat, to simplify, to spend some time with myself. After seeing Siddhartha's lecture, I kept telling myself, silently, over and over, like a mantra, *I want to go inside the belly of the whale.*

The other moment happened before I went to work at Barneys, but it resonated with me during those painful few months when I tried to figure out how leaving Barneys could be an empowered move instead of a defeated one. First, I had seen a story about model Stella Tennant's house in Scotland in *Vogue.* It's a dream house by most anyone's standards—it's in beautiful countryside, it's big but not massive, and it's decorated in a romantic and cozy way. But most appealing and seductive was this idea that she could live there with her husband and her children for everyday life and then jet off to Paris to walk in the Chanel show or fly to New York to make an appearance at the Met Ball. I loved the idea that she could have this quiet, civilized, peaceful life but with occasional doses of glamour and excitement. Then I actually saw Stella at a cocktail party. As we'd met a few times before and have some friends in common, we eventually gravitated toward each other, and I had the chance to ask her about her family life in rural Scotland. Her telling of the quieter pace, the joy of the outdoors, the simplicity of their days, and the thrill of the occasional trip to the city all confirmed what it was I was craving. Further fueled by the example of her well-balanced life, I promised myself I would live like this one day—I just didn't know when. The moment would come sooner than I expected.

When I married a Brit, people always asked me if moving to England was in our near, middle, or distant future. Christopher's family farm is in North Oxfordshire, seven hundred acres stretching across the most beautiful part of the Cotswolds with nineteenth-century stone buildings that have hand-riven slate tiles on the roofs. Christopher's grandfather had bought the farm after the Second World War, and both he and Christopher's father became gentlemen farmers. He and his two siblings had each been given a

home on the farm, and Christopher had created a perfect country cottage. But my reply was always the same: "I don't have to think about it because Christopher never would." He'd made it very clear to me when we first started dating that he was a converted New Yorker through and through. This panicked me a bit because I wasn't sure about New York City at that time.

Years later, after Christopher and I had gotten married, moved to a loft on Chrystie Street (that Christopher had bought way before Whole Foods, the Box, or Freemans had made the area trendy), and my career had taken off, I remember thinking to myself that finally I, too, couldn't imagine living anywhere but New York City.

But in September 2009, Christopher and I were sitting around the dinner table with our friends Hugo, Elliot, and Miranda when the conversation turned to the ongoing recession. It was something Hugo (who is English) said to Christopher and Miranda (also English) that caught my attention. "Well, we all came to New York to build businesses and to be successful, and if there is not much success to be had at the moment, maybe it's time we go back to the wonderful quality of life we had in England. Maybe it's time to enjoy the success we've had so far and stop trying to get more." To my amazement, Christopher replied, "Maybe you're right."

I spent hours thinking in bed that night, *Is this my chance to try living outside of New York?* New experiences have always energized me, and as happy as I was in our home city, I felt a longing to know what else was out there, to look at life from another perspective. Would Christopher really consider moving to England? At that point, I'd learned to really love it. It felt like my homeland. Everything there felt familiar to me—Christopher's mother had the same china pattern that my mother had chosen for the house we grew up in. They sang the same hymns in church. The reserved politeness was already something I was used to, having grown up around people with similar qualities. And I had eventually come to love the farm.

The first few summers I had visited the farm, I was lost there. Christopher was back and forth between houses, but the one we

spent the most time in was the house he and his ex-wife had lived in. They converted it from a cart shed into a cottage, made a beautiful garden, and did the house up in romantic English countryside style. The whole thing was lovely, but it felt too connected to the past for me to really enjoy. Also, Christopher spent his days as a farmer would—trimming hedges, on a tractor, digging trenches, mowing long expanses of grass, and chainsawing fir trees he didn't like. I resolved to teach myself to cook, which was fun, but also quite lonely when done on my own. It didn't get any better when Coco was first born. We brought her there for the month of August when she was just three weeks old. I had no idea what I was doing as a new mom, and I struggled to accept the fact that Christopher found it so easy to spend much of the day outside doing farm chores while I felt trapped in newborn world. From his perspective, that was all he knew. The men worked outside on the farm and the woman took care of all matters relating to the house and the household. We'd hang out in the morning and the evening, but the rest of the day was business as usual. My solution was to have constant houseguests to keep me company, but that strategy became exhausting in a different way.

As Coco got a little bigger, it became apparent that she was in love with horses. That was when everything changed for me at the farm. On our summer visits we'd spend hours, days, weeks grooming the ponies and taking them out for rides. When she was napping I would pull weeds up from the garden and then make a delicious family supper. Having Coco gave me a partner in crime and got me outside doing fun activities that I wouldn't have had the courage or motivation to do on my own. When my son, Zach, came along, the farm was the only place where it felt easy to have two young kids. They were free to roam outside, far away from city streets and cars. We ate healthily, slept well, and had both time to go on adventures and time to be bored. Who has time to get bored in New York City? When Zach was five, he said to me, "Mommy. I love England."

"Why do you love England?" I asked.

"Because it's the only place where I feel free," he responded sincerely.

This feeling of blissful family happiness increased every time we returned to England. Friends would come visit and tell us we were crazy not to live there, and we'd cry each time we left. But were we ready to move to England full time? As the 2009 dinner conversation continued, we decided that no, we weren't ready. I think we were both worried that if we went, we'd never come back. It might feel great for a few years, but then what would we do for the rest of our lives?

My conversation with Christopher about moving to England came up again over Christmas break in 2011. In contemplating my next move after Barneys, I realized that for the first time in seven years, I would have no obligations to anyone—employees, clients, payroll—other than myself. I also had no idea what I wanted to do next in my career. I'd been on a whirlwind of accepting opportunities and experiences that came my way, but I hadn't really been in the driver's seat. I hadn't been planning my future as much as just

Our farm cottage in Oxfordshire, England.

275

saying yes to other people's vision of what my future could be. I felt that I could go on like this indefinitely, just responding to what was put in front of me, but ultimately it wasn't satisfying enough. I missed being creative. I missed expressing my own ideas about fashion and style. I missed writing my book and my blog. I felt like I was living only within small parts of myself and ignoring the rest.

I was in the bath one night, at home on Chrystie Street, and I realized that if I really had any intention of living outside of New York City, for even just a short while, the time was now. My kids were at the right age, and though my husband had obligations in New York, they were nothing that couldn't be taken care of with an occasional visit.

Minutes later, Christopher came into the bathroom while I was brushing my teeth. I put the brush down, swished some water around in my mouth, and said, "Sweetheart, I keep having this fantasy of us living in England. Just for a year. We could go when the kids get out of school, spend the summer getting settled in, and then stay for the kids' school year. I could write my next book, and you could really focus on your painting."

"We could do that . . ." he said, surprising even himself with his lack of resistance. Christopher wondered aloud why, if we were going to take a year off from our lives, we weren't going on a bigger adventure, to Saigon or something. But I didn't want an adventure. I wanted to be calm and peaceful and reflective. I'd had enough upheaval. Also, I knew I would be happy in England, whereas the other places we briefly considered couldn't guarantee that for me. And so that was it. Of course we talked it over and over and spent time independently thinking it through before we made it official, but the course to England was pretty straight from there. We just kept taking the next step forward, albeit quietly and a little nervously.

It wouldn't be until a few months after I left Barneys that the real reason I quit became clear to me. I'd left the job on March 15, exactly a year and a month after my first day there.

A journalist from the *New York Times* had called to propose writing a story about me giving up my coveted, high-profile fashion job for a year off on a farm. Immediately I was cautious and scared. I knew from experience that it was nearly impossible to have a personal story written in the press without some form of deep disappointment attached to something I said or being misunderstood. I felt that I had gotten over the hurdle of leaving Barneys without causing too much drama, so why risk bringing it all up again? Why risk leaving this chapter of two wonderful decades I had spent in New York on a bad note? But the journalist was determined to write the story with or without my participation—yikes!—so I realized this was a challenge I would have to face.

In preparation for our meeting, the journalist repeated a conversation she'd had about me that brought my entire past year into sharp focus.

"Amanda, your former boss [from WME] Mark Dowley says you are the most balanced person he knows. He says that the way you balance your work, your children, your husband, your home, your health, and your whole life is down to an enviable science."

Right then I knew that Mark had generously articulated the very thing that meant the most to me in the world—balance. While I was at Barneys, I had let that balance completely disappear. It wasn't possible for me to do that job and maintain my family life or my home or my friendships the way I always had. It wasn't the responsibilities of the job themselves that caused so much stress. It was the fact that I missed Zach's birthday because it fell during Paris Fashion Week, and I knew I'd always miss it if I stayed on that path. It was because Coco could never understand why I didn't eat dinner with her anymore. It was because the two herniated discs in my back that had started to bother me before I went to Barneys became prohibitively worse when I was there, culminating in the Paris disaster and the spinal steroid injections that followed. It was because I had abandoned my own creative voice following the success of *I Love Your Style* and the creation of

my blog. I had given up so much that was meaningful to me that I didn't feel like myself anymore.

Perhaps the worst regret was when I'd missed a week of work due to my back injury, and then two weeks after I had returned, Zach was diagnosed with pneumonia. He wouldn't have to be hospitalized, the doctor told me, as long as I brought him to the doctor's office twice a day for oxygen treatments. To fit these into my workday, I scheduled them early in the morning and late in the evening (not convenient times for a sick child) so that I could leave him with his nanny and go to work for a full day in between. I still struggle with myself for dragging him out of the house at inappropriate times and not staying home with him when he was the sickest he'd ever been in his life, just because I didn't feel I could miss any more work. To be fair, I didn't ask for the time off. When I was in charge of my own work life, I wouldn't have hesitated to miss any professional opportunity to be home with my seriously ill child, but in this instance I didn't have it in me to explain myself again. My weakness was no one's fault but my own, but it was not the Amanda that I wanted to be.

Besides packing, renting out our apartment, updating passports, securing visas, and saying good-bye to practically everyone we'd ever met in New York, the last hurdle was getting through the *New York Times* interview in a sincere, positive, and humble way. I consulted trusted friends and family, tried to get the closest to the truth in my own heart about my reasons for leaving my job and moving out of the country, and then spent some time alone just thinking about the way I wanted to present myself and explain my current state of mind.

The article was posted online the night before it appeared on newsstands. I knew this because I got an e-mail on the way to our good-bye party with the subject line "New York Times article." It was from Dana Lorenz, the designer of Fenton/Fallon jewelry. The e-mail simply said, "You go girl. This is *your time!*" I felt immediate relief, but I still needed to see it for myself before I knew if I was in the clear.

I stood outside in the rain on my iPhone reading the article before heading inside to my friend's apartment. I got through the whole of it without too much shame, disappointment, or embarrassment. As with all things written about me, I would have changed a few things here and there, but I knew enough to feel lucky for the simple fact that, essentially, they had portrayed me as I'd wanted to be seen.

With all of that behind me, there was nothing left to do but make it to the airport with our dog and all our luggage! I haven't regretted for a moment the decision to take a break from the world that had been mine for so long and to have an experience that would give me a new point of view.

At home on Chrystie Street, NYC, shortly before we moved, in a Proenza Schouler T-shirt and J Brand jeans.

SELF-NOURISHING

SOULCYCLE

I know you're probably laughing at me right now, but—truth be told—the spiritual guidance that led me through my challenging year at Barneys came from a dark sweaty room with pounding nightclub music. There were barely six inches to walk (sideways) between the stationary bikes that filled up the room, and candles were the only light that guided the way to my reserved bike. Seven A.M. was the only class I could fit in my schedule, and I would go every Tuesday and Thursday to ride that bike to the beat of the perfectly curated music and listen as my teacher Danny's wisdom, enthusiasm, and passion guided me into the day. The class was so intense that it was impossible to think about anything other than where I was in that moment, and the resulting high lasted for hours. To have an experience like this before I went into work gave me the feeling of owning my day, of taking the best part of the morning for myself before going out and giving to work, to my career, to other people.

A WATER VIEW

Another thing that created sanity for me throughout my time in New York and my career is nature, specifically water. I moved around a lot when I first arrived in the city full time, and the street I lived on where I finally felt settled had a view of the Hudson River at the end of the block. Coming home each workday to see the early-evening light shining off the surface of the river gave me a sense of psychological release, of freedom that I hadn't felt thus far in the city. Later, when I would move into a family-size apartment on the Lower East Side, I was very worried about losing my evening glimpse of water. But shortly after, we got a little weekend house on Long Island, right on the Sound. Sitting on the beach watching the water and listening to the waves made the two-hour drive out and back, even if just for the day, worth it. Sometimes we would arrive late on a Friday night, long after dark, and after putting the kids in their beds, I would walk down to the beach in the dark and listen to the water. The sounds washed all the stress of the week off my mind.

The view from the top of the lighthouse steps that I climb for exercise when I'm at our summer house in Southold, New York.

HERE ARE many reasons that I value my friends who are artists, but speaking strictly from a style perspective, my time spent around them has been sartorially very liberating. Unlike fashion people, artists are trying to be *different* from the rest of the pack. They are far less self-conscious in using clothes to define themselves, and the resulting look is often far more considered and personal than just piling on the latest trends. My friend Yvonne is the girl I know who is the least scared of embracing a total look. She sees fashion and clothes as if they are a statement by the designer, and she is very respectful of maintaining the integrity of that expression. While most girls I know want to change the look to make it their own, Yvonne's own look is about choosing the look that is right for her and embracing it as faithfully as she can. Rachel's style, on the other hand, is more focused on her iconic body, hair, and face. As an artist herself and as the muse of her husband, John Currin, Rachel's look—if it can even be defined—is buxom bombshell with a vintage sexy-secretary vibe thrown in. It suits her entirely and no one else looks like her. Isn't that what we all aspire to? Then there's Anh. She knows herself so well. She is probably the most exotic-looking friend I have. Her face is so exquisite that she would look great no matter what she was wearing. It is for

that reason that she embraces simple, classic clothes that let her physical features do all the talking. As glamorous as she looks dressed up at night, I am most inspired when I catch a glimpse of her in an apron and clogs in her painting studio. And finally, Inez, a photographer, is another striking-looking woman, and she wears a daily uniform that is practical for photo shoots and flattering to her figure. She wore New Balance sneakers every day long before it was cool to do so, and in the evening she'll dress up her jeans and T-shirt with a fur jacket and high-heeled boots. To me, her look says, "I am the coolest girl in high school," and I bet she was.

Opposite, clockwise from top left:
Yvonne Force Villareal; me, Rachel
Feinstein, and Yvonne; Rachel;
Inez Van Lamsweerde; Anh Duong.

A YEAR ON THE FARM:
MAKING JAM IS
THE BEST REVENGE

I'M SURE it will take me many years to understand the full extent of why moving to England was so good for me, just like I am *still* processing why it eventually came to be that living in New York at that time in my life had become untenable. But the fact is that I am happy here, on a much simpler but deeper level than I could have imagined for myself. I have never been more certain of who I am and what is important to me. There is enough time and space here to listen to myself—my mind *and* my body. I know when it's time to work hard and when it's time to rest. The tension is gone from my shoulders, and the adrenaline that lived inside my belly for twenty years in New York has settled down. I know it because whenever I go back to New York, the rush returns and I notice it now because I'm less used to it—it's a foreign feeling. My husband is as happy as I am, for similar reasons. And my kids are thriving. *Thriving.*

For the first year here (it's now been nearly three!), I really did just allow myself to unwind and to find a new balance. The demands of setting up family life in a new country are not easy. My kids had been ripped away from their comfort zone and required thoughtful encouragement and consistent support from me in

Opposite: On the farm in a J.Crew sweatshirt and my trusty Céline sunglasses.

285

finding a new one both at home and at school. Our house had never been a full-time home and needed many improvements to withstand greater use. I had to learn to drive on the wrong side of the road, figure out how to navigate a roundabout, and eventually pass the notoriously challenging British driving test. But I balanced these responsibilities with the more pleasurable pursuits of learning to jump fences on my horse, taking blackberry-picking breaks with my husband in the midafternoon, cooking three meals a day for my family, and discovering the challenges and joys of jam-making. Yes, I really do make jam. First of all, we, as a large extended farm family, could never eat all the fresh fruit that grows on the trees here, but more important, I love the kind of meditative step-by-step method of measuring the fruit and sugar, stirring the mixture slowly over the fire while watching for signs of setting, sterilizing and labeling the jars, tying a bow around the lid, and ultimately giving the finished product as a present to friends. (I've been watching *Scandal* on TV recently, and every time Olivia Pope and the POTUS dream of giving up their high-powered careers to make jam in the countryside, I must admit I get a little whiff of self-satisfaction.)

Laura Bailey and me holding newborn lambs at nearby Daylesford Organic Farm.

And of course, because I'm me—a ball of energy who feels most at home with a schedule and a goal in front of me—I set about to write this book. It's taken longer than I planned because I didn't anticipate so many pleasurable distractions, but still it's held me accountable to my long-term goals and made me feel that I wasn't *just* a farmwife, a country bumpkin, a soccer mom—all titles I am proud to accept for the time being.

When I was sitting in my office at Barneys fantasizing about my impending life on the farm, I imagined having the time to do yoga

regularly and meditate each morning. I imagined creating an art studio for myself, pulling out all the inspiration I have collected over the years and creating something entirely original. Perhaps I'm still unwinding from the addiction to busy days, but I haven't quite found the time for those activities yet. Or maybe I just have to take responsibility for not holding those goals high enough on my priority list.

I do, however, have a long, hot bath before I get into bed every single night. Why didn't I do that in New York? It's such an obvious stress reliever. I also take walks with my dog, Ginger, during which I allow my mind to wander, to see things more clearly, and to process how I ended up here in this place so far away from what I know. I am starting to be able to look at my life in New York City and what I consider to be only the first half of my career, and find some wisdom in the choices I made.

There was a part of me that never forgave myself for giving up photography so quickly when starting out in my twenties. Photography was the truest passion in my life when I emerged from college and moved to New York. Why had I abandoned it at the first chance I got? At the time I was confused about whether to pursue a photography career in fashion or a fine art. And in either case I didn't know what would set me apart from all the other photographers out there whom I loved and was influenced by. But isn't that the struggle of every artist's beginning? As I have thought it through further, I started to think about the conditioning I received from my exceptional education. No question I attended fine academic institutions surrounded by "the best and the brightest" of America's future, but I realized that, over time, I became attached to this idea of being at the top of the pile, ahead of the field. I had the Ivy League diploma, the coveted internships, the drive, the discipline, the ambition. Nothing prepared me for going to New York at the bottom of the pile, for being a struggling artist. Nearly every single one of my school friends had already aligned themselves with prestigious institutions—investment banks, well-known charitable foundations, further education at

Yale or Harvard—to continue their tradition of excellence. And soon I followed suit, quickly giving up my photography dreams to align myself with Gagosian, the most prestigious art gallery in the world. I reconciled this by telling myself that I could always have photography in my life. It didn't have to be my career—it could be my hobby. And maybe one day, when the moment was right, I would return to my pursuit of my greatest creative passion.

And you know what? That part actually turned out to be true. Just when I was leaving New York, I discovered Instagram. I had really struggled with Twitter. I don't find myself to be quippy or clever in 140 characters. But for me, images say everything I feel the urge to express. I started sharing pictures of my unfolding life on the farm, and people have responded to them in the most gratifying way. Taking photographs again has fulfilled a deeply buried craving. I don't know where this pursuit is going yet, whether I will pursue photography as part of my professional life or whether it is destined to remain as my hobby.

In terms of fashion, I have never enjoyed getting dressed more than with the limited options I have here at the farm. This new simplicity has forced me to further define who I am and what I want clothes to say about me. After twenty years of being a fashion chameleon, I finally can say I have the defined sense of my sartorial self that I was always looking for. I have to work harder to make old things seem new by combining them in unexpected ways or changing the proportion. I dress more discreetly than I ever have, but I still take great pride in the quality and design of the things I choose to buy. On the whole, my outfit each day starts with practicality—if my day includes riding, I put on jodhpurs; if not, I usually wear corduroys or jeans that are narrow enough to tuck into boots. I seem to always wear boots here—wellies when it's wet (very often), Portuguese soft leather riding boots when it's dry, or my beautiful custom-made E. Vogel boots (a coming-to-England present from Christopher) if I am planning to get on a horse. Then I'll wear a T-shirt in the summer or a turtleneck or plaid flannel in the winter, topped with a chunky sweater. This

base look pretty much makes me feel like a prep-school girl, and truth be told, that's what I am. I feel at home in this look. But then I always add something chic and current to remind myself of my fashionable alter ego—a Proenza Schouler vest, a Balmain pea coat, my Repossi ring. Sixty percent of what is in my closet these days are classic basics from J.Crew, but I still have the occasional splurge on Isabel Marant when I am in London, and the nearby Céline outlet store (YES! There is a Céline outlet thirty minutes from my house!) has proven a very effective way to relapse into overspending on clothes when the urge overwhelms me.

I have also had the occasional encounters with the fashion industry in wonderfully unexpected ways. After following me on Instagram, my good friend Jenna Lyons rang me up to ask if J.Crew could shoot their catalogue on our farm, and include us in it to boot! I couldn't have been any more flattered or excited. The only bummer is that it turned out Zach and I would be in New York when they came. He had been looking forward to two weeks of summer camp at Chelsea Piers and I didn't have the heart to cancel for a photo shoot. I felt good about my decision (and still do), de-

Giving Zach a hug as Christopher drives us around the farm in an old Land Rover. I live in this Proenza Schouler T-shirt in England.

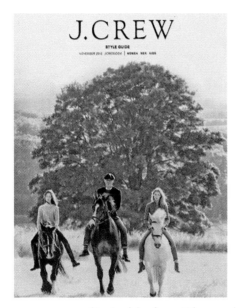

J.CREW
STYLE GUIDE
NOVEMBER 2015 JCREW.COM | WOMEN MEN KIDS

The J.Crew cover featuring Coco and Christopher and some of our horses, shot at the farm, 2013.

spite the extra pang when Christopher and Coco ended up on the cover!

I also recently did a photographic collaboration with Zara. Every month for five months, they would send me a pile of the newest Zara clothes and I would take personal still lifes and self-portraits of the clothes in an environment of my choosing (mostly at the farm). This was particularly satisfying as it included fashion, photography, and the farm—all the elements of the new me. Not to mention that working with Zara brought me happily back to my Contempo Casual days, when my style was defined by a thirst for self-definition through fashion, albeit on a limited budget. These acknowledgments from the fashion world have beautifully brought together my old life with my new one and given me hope that it is possible to integrate fashion back into my world on my own terms.

My least-expected fashion encounter that has happened since I left Barneys was—as Oprah would say—my "full-circle moment" with Patrick Demarchelier. I got a call from art director Doug Lloyd, who was casting real women to be photographed for Bottega Veneta's jewelry line. I accepted, proud to be included in the group of inspiring women (Anh Duong and Garance Doré, among others) he had assembled, and couldn't have been happier when I received the call sheet and discovered that Patrick would be taking my portrait. When the day came, I went back to the same studio I had worked in sixteen years before, and everything was pretty much the same. I sat in the same hair and makeup chairs in front of the same mirrors. And when I walked onto the familiar set, Patrick and I had the giggles for quite some time. Patrick asked me if I wanted to load the film or adjust the lights before we began. And in typical

Patrick fashion, the whole shoot was over in about three minutes. Did I feel important that day? Not really. I felt empowered that I had been chosen in my own right, not because I was representing a company I had worked for. But oddly, I felt much like my twenty-two-year-old self—lucky to be there, happy for the experience.

Speaking of feeling twenty-two again, I often feel that way these days. I am living off a fraction of the salary I made at Barneys, yet my life has never felt more abundant. When I think about the future of my career, I feel I have been given the chance to start over from that right-out-of-college moment, but with the benefit of all I have learned. I have posted a quote I saw on Instagram above my desk. It reads, "If you don't build your dream, someone else will hire you to build theirs." I know I have my own dream in me, and I am using the time I have here on the farm to define and refine it until I am ready to make it come to life. This past year I turned forty. I feel grateful to have so many experiences under my belt, but with a lot of life still ahead of me. Sometimes when I feel anxious to know what the future holds, I remind myself of the many successful woman, like DVF, who have launched or re-launched themselves well into their forties and fifties.

My modeling moment for Bottega Veneta jewelry, 2012.

Right now, I want to be fully present and available to my kids while they are still at home. We don't have a nanny. I get Zach up (Coco is now at boarding school with her horse!) and give him breakfast. Christopher and I share the school run. I make dinner, and we both hang out with him before bedtime. Our increased involvement in life at home (and closer proximity) mean that Christopher and I bicker more than we used to, but we also share

Teaching a hen chick how to fly on the farm, 2014. Photo by Coco Brooks.

such a greater sense of responsibility and pride as parents. We are a team, and I feel closer to him than I ever have. On our occasional night out, Christopher's mother often looks after the kids, or their friends' parents are more than willing to have them over. I can't imagine calling friends in New York and asking them to have my child spend the night during the school week.

I also have come to realize how much I enjoy time alone. I love riding my horse in silence, driving around in my car listening to music, spending long hours in my office with no one to talk to and no phone calls coming in. I don't even have a phone in my office. I now marvel at how I spent nearly two decades in New York with so little time to myself, if any at all.

When Sheryl Sandberg's book, *Lean In*, came out, I couldn't face buying it or reading it, despite the raves from many friends. Why did I feel threatened by the idea of having it all? Was it because I thought that I *couldn't* have it all? Or because I had it all already? While many people would look at my life now and say that I *definitely* have it all—I am so grateful to have a wonderful family, a beautiful farm to live on, self-employment, flexibility—I know that my career has another chapter somewhere in the future. I am a working girl, always have been. What I do realize is that it's possible to have it all, but over a lifetime. Having it all at once? I know myself well enough to say I couldn't enjoy it all piled on simultaneously. Besides, what's the rush? It's nice to have something to look forward to.

MY GREATEST HITS

MY TEN BEST PIECES
OF CLOTHING

Céline Men's Tailored Shirt
As I have a pretty narrow, straight-up-and-down frame, shirts with darts (those seams that transform a masculine-styled shirt into a feminine shape) do not suit me. I like button-down shirts as they were intended—a relaxed shape and perhaps one size too big, as if borrowed from my husband. I also prefer them to be made of a substantial fabric—not too thick—but of enough quality that the collar holds its shape and the cuffs can be casually rolled up and stay in position. In this regard, Céline makes the perfect button-down shirts for me. I have three—all traditional stripes—and in slightly different styles: One has a tab collar, one is longer, and the other is more fitted. I got two of them at the Céline outlet store and the third on sale at Barneys when I worked there. There's nothing to say that my views on men's tailored shirts will be the same as yours, but I believe every woman should

have a well-cultivated point of view on what shirt shape, fabric, and style works best for her body and her look.

Goldsign Jeans
Finally! Finally I have found a jeans brand that looks good, is comfortable (i.e., the right amount of stretch), and has styling that I like (no back pocket decoration or other obvious branding). I first discovered them at J.Crew, when they did a collaboration with the brand. There I bought a pair of perfect cropped white jeans for the summer. White jeans are difficult to get right because, among all the other factors we are all so picky about, they can also be see-through in the wrong places. Despite cutting out the front pockets (I *always* do that with white jeans), these jeans are perfect in all regards. I also recently found a blue pair that are subtly worn in all the right places but with no holes, and they have a great shape—they are narrow and full length, but I wear them with a two-inch roll at the bottom so they

show off my shoes—sandals in the summer, boots in the winter.

Chanel Faux-Crocodile Jacket
When I was in New York, Chanel was my go-to resource for borrowing something fabulous for a party. I know. Lucky me! The Chanel PR girls are so lovely and well mannered, and they always were happy to watch me try on dresses and blouses and accessories and tell me their opinion. Occasionally, I'd get really lucky and be told I could keep a sample piece that I particularly loved that the press office felt they no longer needed. This was how the best jacket I have ever owned fell into my hands. It's a tiny little thing—whenever I first put it on I'm always shocked by how restricting it is. The sleeves are narrow, the armholes are high, and the material—a glazed linen in a croc pattern that looks like printed leather but is not—is unforgiving. But it just looks *so good* on. It's cropped just above the hipbone and it has the most intricate,

294

detailed, and feminine seaming that creates just the slightest hint of a peplum. I have worn this jacket with everything from white jeans and black ballet flats to a vintage Peruvian party skirt and red Louboutin sandals. Whenever I'm going to a party and I need a little something to cover my shoulders, or to dress down a look or to dress up a look, the little Chanel jacket is the perfect thing.

J.Crew Cashmere V-Neck Sweater

Everyone has their sweater shape, and for me it's the V-neck. I like the versatility of wearing it with nothing underneath for a sexier look, and with a collared shirt underneath for a tomboy look. I always buy the same shape from J.Crew—it's traditional and straightforward—and in a women's size large. As with men's-styled shirts, I like the loose-fitting casual look. I tend to choose my sweaters in neutral colors—gray, navy, oatmeal—although this winter I went with teal. I

was thrilled with the color at first but quickly grew tired of it—which reminds me that when buying things that are classic (meaning I plan to keep them in my closet for at least five years), it's best to stick with classic colors. These are my basics, so they need to be versatile. There are plenty of other areas—shoes, bag, shirt—to get my hit of fashion impact if need be.

Balmain Army Green Pea Coat

I knew I was leaving Barneys a couple of months before I actually got up the courage to resign. I was acutely aware that once I left, I'd be leaving a big salary behind and I would have to live *way* more frugally than I was used to, especially as I was planning to move to England and didn't have any immediate work plans. So I put myself on a shopping moratorium. After a year of free-for-all shopping with my healthy discount, I told myself not to buy one more thing and start saving. Now. But then I saw this jacket. I had been admiring it for

months. It was an army green wool military pea coat by Balmain, and it was more than $5,000. Now that's just silly money. Even if I had all the money in the world, I don't think I could bring myself to spend that much money on a wool coat. But I kept my eye on it, thinking that most people in their right mind would agree with me, and perhaps it would go on sale. Sale time came and the coat price went down by 40 percent. Combined with my 35 percent discount, it would still come to $1,950. Not doing it. A month later, it went down to 50 percent off. Still not enough. Then, the final week that I was at work, I got a message from my salesperson saying that the coat had been reduced to 75 percent off. Faced with the possibility of getting a $5,000 coat for just over $800, I was seduced but still not convinced. I had promised myself I wouldn't buy another thing. But then I thought of all those cold, rainy, foggy autumn and winter days I'd face in England. And how many of

my beautiful clothes I'd have to give away or leave behind in storage in New York as I ventured off on my new farm life with very limited closet space. And I thought of how perfectly this one piece of stunning yet discreet design would fit into my English lifestyle and dress up the jeans, plaid shirt, and wellies. I knew I'd be likely to wear it every day. So I bought the coat. It's been everything I hoped it would be and more. I've worn it to the school run, to London for meetings, to shoot weekends at friends' houses, for Sunday walks, and it's always kept me just one step away from feeling like the country bumpkin I've become.

Proenza Schouler T-Shirts

If you're a young fashion design brand, and you're smart, you know you have to design certain items within your collection that become your "bread and butter"— the seasonal basics that become staples in a woman's wardrobe long after the trends have moved on, and that keep them coming back

for more. For most brands, it's a tailored trouser or a signature cardigan, but in the case of Proenza Schouler, they found longevity in a printed T-shirt. Each season they take the one print, stripe, or design that sums up what the fashion season is about for them, and they put it on a T-shirt. It's a casual way of acknowledging the season's trend without breaking the bank. One season it's tie-dye, then it's stripes, then it's a Navajo print, then it's zigzags. Over time I have managed to build up a little collection of these T-shirts, and they remain front and center in my closet year after year. I find them so useful. As most of my clothes these days are neutral in color and classic in cut, my PS T-shirts add just a touch of personality when I am in danger of being too safe and boring.

My Alaïa Skirt

Another splurge—but one I don't regret—from my Barneys days. I never thought of myself as a person who would walk into a store

and buy something from Azzedine Alaïa. Of course, I am huge fan and admirer, but I just hadn't ever been able to relate to being able to afford to spend *that much* on any one piece of clothing. But there I was at Barneys, a few months into the job, and my paycheck had just arrived. I had gotten through the first month of fashion shows, had settled into my new routine, and wanted to reward myself with something *good*. I can't tell you how much fun it was to walk through the store having given myself the permission to indulge. I knew I wasn't going to go crazy and buy a fur or some over-the-top embellished piece, but I knew I was looking for *an investment piece*, let's say. First I went to Céline, my favorite brand, but all the best pieces there were classic basics and I wanted to buy something that made an *impact*. After looking over the racks throughout the store, I came to the Alaïa section. His fall collection that year was particularly good. I loved the ultrafeminine shapes done in

more masculine colors like burgundy and hunter green. My eye landed on a skirt in hunter green and black zebra stripe. I can't tell you what the fabric was other than that it was a lush, stretchy woven knit that felt like velvet when I touched it. The shape was fitted from the waist and over the hips and then flared out toward the hem, hitting just below my knee. It was the most luxurious and feminine thing I had ever put on my body. I *loved* it, and I have never regretted buying it for a second. I have it here with me in England and I actually wear it more here than I did in New York. With a silk camisole and my Chanel jacket, it's perfect for a fashion event in London; with a chunky sweater, it's great for a cozy Saturday night dinner in the country; and with a black turtleneck and flat, black jodhpurs, it's great for a day of meetings. I hope it lasts forever.

J.Crew Mid-Rise Toothpick Cords

It wasn't until I moved to England that I had a use for any kind of pants in between jeans and formal trousers. But here, it's not quite the same—of course I spend *a lot* of time in jeans, and I hardly ever wear formal trousers, but I have a huge use for something that looks a bit more put together than jeans but is still casual. At first, the question of where to fulfill this need totally stumped me. I knew J.Crew had great colored cords, but in the past I could never find the shape that fit me—they were either too big in the waist or too short. But out of desperation I decided to give them another chance. What I found was that they had completely reinvented their pant shapes and styles to suit more women. For me, perfection was found in the mid-rise toothpick. The waist covers my belly button (as I like it to), and they fit well through the butt and thighs. The ankle is narrow, and the hem hits at the perfect place to easily tuck into a knee-length boot or fall just above an ankle boot. And the colors! Every season, there are a dozen colors and I am usually tempted to buy them all, even though I choose just one or two.

Phillip Lim Embroidered Evening Cape

One of my great fashion lessons learned over the years is that sometimes something decorative and over the top can be just as classic as something basic. A few years back, I was sitting in the front row of the Phillip Lim runway show when I clocked this cape walking past me. It was black, had slits for the hands to pass through, and the length hit just around mid-calf. It moved in the most elegant way. But then as it passed under one of the spotlights just in front of me, I noticed that the whole thing was embroidered with a black ribbon in an elaborate floral design. That was when I began to drool. Days later, as I made my usual showroom visit, I told Phillip right away that I had to see *that cape*! It looked like something I could never afford—if I'd seen it on the street I would have assumed it was Oscar de la Renta and cost $25,000.

For real. But that's the brilliance of Phillip's clothes. He makes beautiful, intricate things affordable. Of course it wasn't cheap—I think with my friends-and-family wholesale discount at the showroom it was $600—but I wear it every winter to any formal occasion I have, and I am always sad when I arrive and have to leave it at the door. When I do encounter other women while wearing it, they swoon, too. It's just one of those drool-worthy things that I feel lucky to have discovered.

Whatever Floral-Print Dress I Have Hanging Around That Season

Truth be told, I don't buy much pattern or print—I prefer to invest in things that I won't grow sick of. But often in the summer I inevitably stumble upon a floral dress—usually in a bohemian shape—that just shouts my name. Recently it's been an Étoile by Isabel Marant (her cheaper line) dress, but Thakoon and Phillip Lim have made some of my favorites as well. I don't

necessarily buy one every year, and I often bring old ones back into rotation when they look new to me again, but whatever the chosen dress of that season is, I tend to wear it until I can't bear to look at it again, and it gets put away until its appeal comes back to me. Or not.

FIVE BEST ACCESSORIES

Céline Sunglasses

I have two pairs—black and tortoiseshell. They are both the same style—a version of a Wayfarer that is slightly bigger and with slightly harder edges. A modern classic.

Manolo Blahnik BB Pumps

I have had two pairs of these in black and brown suede since the late nineties. They sat untouched in my closet for many years while I was more attracted to chunkier shoes and platforms, and then in 2010 they came back out again. These days, whenever I consider shoes to wear with a dress, it's rare that anything looks chicer or more timeless than these.

Proenza Schouler Colorblocked PS1 Bag

When Proenza Schouler launched a handbag collection, they hit the ball right out of the park with the PS1 bag. I love its lack of bells and whistles, and its utilitarian shape. In the evening, I carry the clutch style in navy suede, but it's my colorblocked day bag in natural linen, brown leather, and black suede that gets carried more than any other bag in my closet.

Chanel Maxi 2.55 Bag

This bag was a very generous gift from Chanel when I did my first book tour with them. It's the largest version of the classic quilted 2.55 bag with a metal chain—prefect for fitting in your iPad and a magazine on top of your daily stuff—and it's in a very dark teal lambskin, which feels more unique to me than all the black ones I see around. It's my most coveted accessory.

Repetto Flats

Leave it to Kate Moss to have led me to my favorite everyday shoe—when I first noticed her wearing the perfect ballet flat, with the perfect roundness in the toe, the perfect amount of coverage on the foot, and the perfect relaxed shape, I had to search high and low in Paris to find the store that sold them. But I was hooked. Now, years later, you can get Repetto flats on most corners of both Paris and New York, but I still love them. They are perfect right when you buy them, and they get even better with age. They come in a million colors and materials, and the fit is always the same. My daughter likes to tell me that she is "so over" ballet flats, but I don't think I will ever be.

THANK YOU

To Sarah Hochman, for understanding me so completely.
The first time I met you, I knew I wanted you to edit my next book.

To Simon Doonan for the introduction to Sarah. You were spot-on.

To Richard Pandiscio, for taking on round two.

To Bill Loccisano, for your focused and dedicated hard work, the beautiful results,
and for knowing me well enough to laugh at me.

To everyone at Blue Rider Press and Penguin Random House who had a hand
in bringing this book to life: David Rosenthal, Phoebe Pickering, Joanna Kamouh,
Aileen Boyle, Brian Ulicky, Eliza Rosenberry, and Claire Vaccaro.

To David Kuhn, Jessie Borkan, William LoTurco, and Nicole Tourtelot for dreaming big on my behalf.

To DVF, for being such a devoted champion. I am forever grateful for your love, wisdom, and support.

To all of my former bosses—Patrick Demarchelier, Larry Gagosian, Frédéric Fekkai, Diego Della Valle,
Emanuele Della Valle, Josh Patner, Bryan Bradley, Mark Dowley, Jay Fielden, Daniella Vitale, and Mark Lee—
for choosing me and for sharing your success and knowledge with me.

To Anna Wintour, for including me in your incredible world.

To Laura Stoloff, Chelsea Fairless, and Phoebe Cutter, for being the determined young women
I had in mind while writing this book.

To Kimberly Cutter, for setting the bar high and for sharing the benefit
of your writing and editing genius with me.

To Regena Thomashauer, for encouraging my every move.
And for dragging my ass to SoulCycle in my darkest moments.

To my early readers—Eve MacSweeney, Kimberly Cutter, Amy Astley, Taylor Tomasi Hill,
Laura Stoloff, Sarah Geary, and Laura Bailey—for your suggestions and encouragement.

To Jackie Skye Kim, for your invaluable help in research and permissions.

To the friends and places that have enabled my writing: Rebekah Brooks (SHA),
Rose Van Cutsem (the Village Pub), Bella Pollen & Co. (Westwell),
and the staff at Daylesford Farm Shop café, Turl Street Kitchen,
and the Bodleian Library, Oxford.

To Robin Bellinger, for telling me to keep writing when I was having serious doubts.

And finally to my parents—all three of you—for your love.

IMAGE CREDITS

JIL SANDER

AMANDA BROOKS
GA13

Ground Floor Ab 69

Amanda Brooks

Womenswear Show
Fall/Winter 2011

PRADA

Aa 36

DRIES VAN NOTEN

WOMEN'S COLLECTION WINTER 2011-2012
WEDNESDAY 2ND MARCH 2011 AT 3PM

Mrs Amanda Brooks.

3 RUE DE LOBAU   75004 PARIS
METRO: HOTEL DE VILLE

COMMUNICATIONS: +33-1-42 74 44 07

Lincoln Center   *Amanda Brook*

FASHION'S NIGHT OUT
THE SHOW
Tuesday, September 7, 2010 7:30 PM, Rain or Shine
Josie Robertson Plaza Columbus Avenue between 62nd and 65th Sts
Doors Open at 6:00 PM, Close at 7:15 PM, No Late Seating
No Large Bags/Backpacks, Still/Video Cameras, or Umbrellas

Entrance	Side	Section	Row	Seat
Broadway at 65th St	NORTH	1	B	4

...Collection
...remps-Été 2012
15 rue Cassette, Paris 6ème
Le Jeudi 29 Septembre 2011 à 10h00.
Madame Amanda Brooks
D 75

KENZO
PARIS

*Amanda
Brooks*

FLOOR 4 | MORNING GLORY BLUE

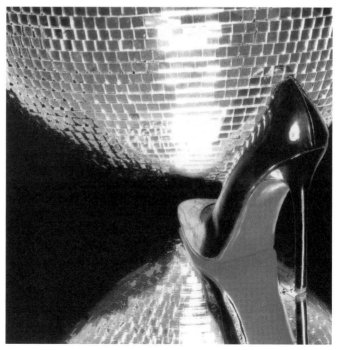